HIP LOUNGING

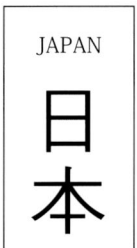

JAPAN
日本

LINKS

First published in 2008 by
Page One Publishing Private Limited
20 Kaki Bukit View
Kaki Bukit Techpark II
Singapore 415956
Tel: (65) 6742-2088
Fax: (65) 6744-2088
enquiries@pageonegroup.com
www.pageonegroup.com

Editorial/Creative Director
Kelley Cheng

Editor
Elaine Lee

Author
Ellen Nepilly

Graphic Designer & Editorial Coordinator
Adelien Vandeweghe

Japanese Copywriter
Junichi Yanagisawa

Translator of Japanese Copywriting
Ellen Nepilly

Proofreader
Joyce Sim

Japanese proofreaders: **Yoshiyuki Yamaguchi & Suthatip Yaiyiam**

All rights reserved. No part of this publication may be reproduced, stored in any retrieval system or transmitted, in any form or by any means, electronic, mechanical, photocopying, recording or otherwise, without prior permission in writing from the publisher.
For information, contact Page One Publishing Private Limited, 20 Kaki Bukit View, Kaki Bukit Techpark II, Singapore 415956.

Printed and bound in China

HIP LOUNGING JAPAN
Copyright © 2008 Page One Publishing Private Limited

First published in Europe 2008 by:
Linksbooks
Jonqueres, 10, 1-5
08003 Barcelona, Spain
Tel: +34 93 301 21 99
Fax: +34 93 301 00 21
E-mail: info@linksbooks.net
www.linksbooks.com

Distributed by:
Linksbooks
Jonqueres, 10, 1-5
08003 Barcelona, Spain
Tel: +34 93 301 21 99
Fax: +34 93 301 00 21

ISBN 978-84-96263-92-5

HIP LOUNGING

JAPAN
日本

ELLEN NEPILLY

LINKS

目次 *Contents*

006	Introduction	098	B bar Umeda
008	Velours	104	Estasi
014	Le Baron de Paris	108	Club Bisser
020	Absolut Icebar	114	Le Cinq
024	Danceteria Sazae	118	Luxe Bar Eats
028	Kita Aoyama Salon	124	Thunderbolt
032	Remix	130	Bar R
036	Birth	136	Stair
040	Minerva	142	Water Drops
044	Shichi-Zo	146	Den Aquaroom
048	Zazzle	152	Shizuku To Ya
052	Shimuraya	156	Yamazaki
056	Amebar	160	Blue Lounge
060	Live & Bar 11	164	Ku-zu-ku
064	Zodiac	168	Mission
068	Le Cabaret	174	Suikyo-tei
074	Club Zoo	180	Yururi
080	Euro Café	186	Restaurants: Addresses
084	Rosa	188	Architects & Designers: Index
088	Seaside	190	Poems: Translations
092	Sakuraji	192	Acknowledgements

序章 *Introduction*

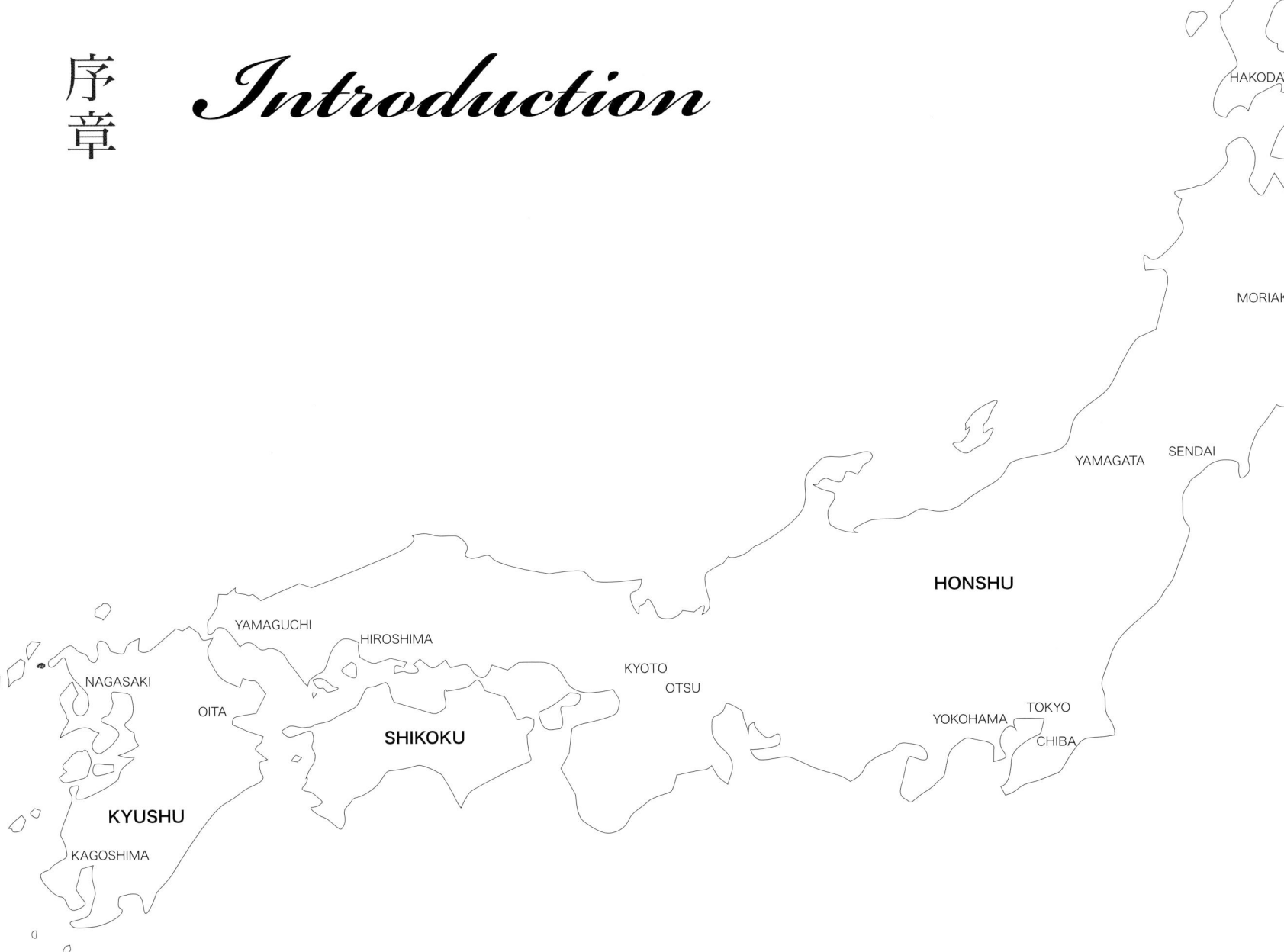

Nightlife in Japan is as extraordinary and as diverse as it could possibly be. In Japan's densely populated cities where people often live in tiny apartments and many need to commute long distances to dormitory villages, the buzz is where the workplaces are. Going out for a drink after work is common practice; hence the selection of locations to spend the evening is enormous. To remain competitive in a country where good service is standard and not really something that can be advertised, hip design interiors have become an important means of luring customers who are looking for an aesthetic experience.

Hip Lounging Japan showcases a selection of some of the most extraordinary lounge interiors Japan has to offer. It not only introduces strikingly trendy design, but also explains different aspects of Japan and Japanese culture. This book not only features a great selection of the hippest contemporary lounge bars, nightclubs, girls' bars and hostess clubs of Japan's major metropolitan areas, but also highlights a variety of places located in remoter areas, ranging from Sendai City situated north of Tokyo, to the subtropical prefecture of Okinawa in the East China Sea.

東京

ベロア

Velours

Strutting the glass catwalk

With its many designer shops, galleries, stylish restaurants and clubs, the trendy Tokyo neighbourhood of Minami Aoyama offers many possibilities for a night out, with Velours being one of the fanciest. At the entrance, a pine tree bonsai welcomes its guests. Walking through the automatic front door, clubbers can admire the mirror art of artist Daisuke Nakayama on the wall of the hallway, created specially for Velour's interior.

The 35 m glass catwalk over an illuminated bird relief dividing the lounge area and the dance floor is another highlight, constructed such that guests from every seat can view it. The bird relief is carved into Styrol and then coated with sand. Fashion shows and other events regularly held at Velours make full use of the catwalk.

With a balanced fusion of classic and modern, as well as Western and Japanese styles, the club's interior is the perfect place for stylish Tokyoites. Stuffed peacocks, crystal chandeliers and the stuffed head of a buffalo do not appear too extravagant alongside the white catwalk reflected in ceiling mirrors and the rather classic grey furniture. A red sofa and gorgeously-lit front counter in red enhance the rest of the dark interior.

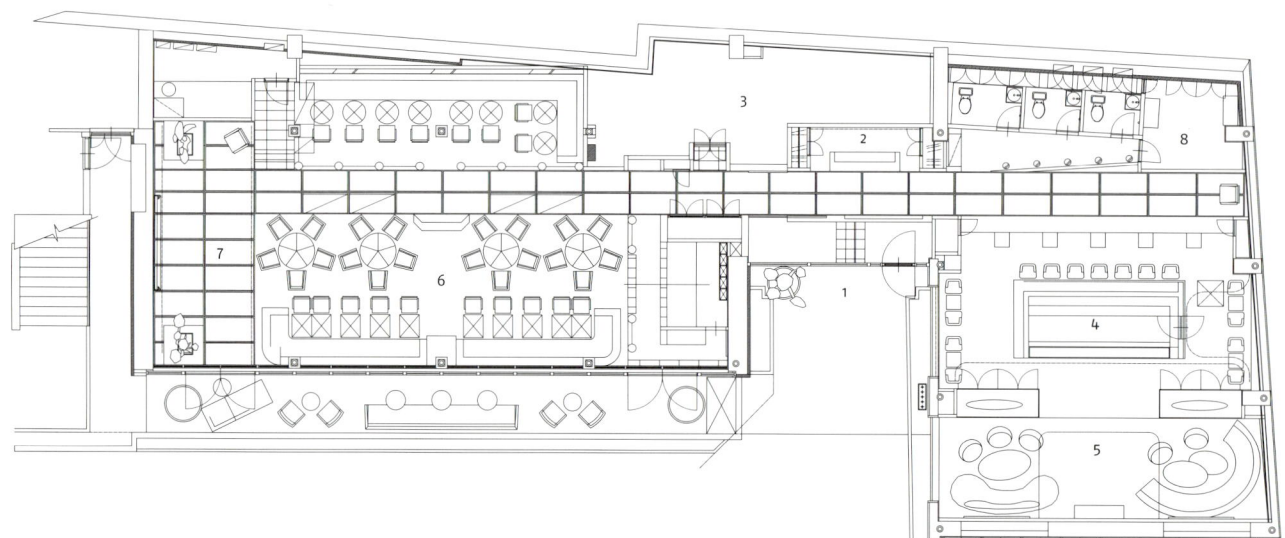

FLOORPLAN

1. entrance
2. reception
3. staff room
4. bar
5. VIP lounge
6. main lounge
7. stage
8. washroom

古今和洋を対峙させ融合させる、ここはここだけの異空間。

PHOTOGRAPHY	Takeshi Nakasa (Nacasa & Partners Inc.)
DESIGNER	design room 702
DESIGN TEAM	Hiroyuki Matsunaka
CONTRACTOR	Ing. Styler, Inc.
ADDRESS	Orumosuto-Blue B1, 6-4-6 Minami-Aoyama, Minato-ku, Tokyo 107-0062
PHONE	+81 (0) 3 5778 4777
AREA	356 m²
SEATING	93 seats
COMPLETED	2004

東京

ル バロン ド パリ

Le Baron de Paris

Red velvet on bare skin

A sister club of Le Baron, the famously exclusive Parisian VIP nightclub, has descended on the Tokyo nightlife scene. Offering space for a maximum of 200 people - obviously a small number in Tokyo – clubbers must either be invited, famous or just plain lucky to get in. A fantastic interior and funky music await the happy ones who do.

The entrance area and the wall of the staircase leading down to the main floor are designed after the Parisian landscape, with an image of the Eiffel Tower and paintings of Parisian buildings. Upon walking in, guests are greeted by three bare behinds.

These belong to naked female models on a gorgeous old black and white photograph hanging over a gigantic brown leather couch in one of the seating areas. Those more interested in art than in other guests can enjoy other equally interesting photographs throughout the interior.

A huge, partially isolated VIP room is equipped with plush blood red velvet couches and red lighting. From there, guests can see the DJ, dance floor, and the counter. Australian-born designer Marc Newson designed two special karaoke VIP rooms where the most elite guests can enjoy their corner of privacy in the club.

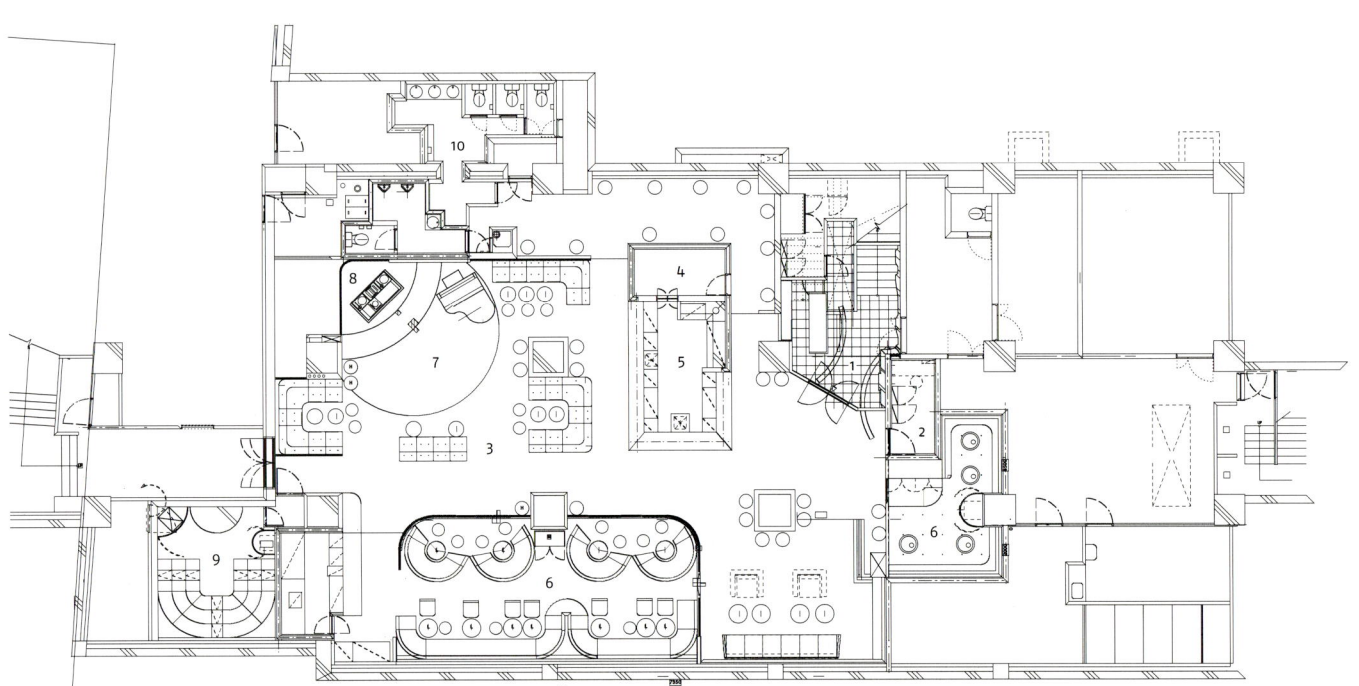

FLOORPLAN

1. entrance
2. staff room
3. lounge area
4. kitchen
5. bar
6. VIP lounge
7. dance floor
8. DJ
9. karaoke room
10. washroom

真紅と漆黒。悠久の貴族に捕われ、もう一人の自分に出会う。

PHOTOGRAPHY	Takeshi Nakasa (Nacasa & Partners Inc.)
DESIGNER	design room 702
DESIGN TEAM	Hiroyuki Matsunaka
CONTRACTOR	Vithmic Tokyo
ADDRESS	Aoyama Center Bldg. B1F 3-8-40, Minami-Aoyama, Minato-ku, Tokyo 108-0072
PHONE	+81 (0) 3 3408 3665
AREA	410 m²
SEATING	88 seats
COMPLETED	2006

Absolut Icebar

Tokyo's coolest bar

東京 アブソルート アイスバー

To escape the oppressing heat of Tokyo's summer, this bar offers the perfect refuge. With an all year round temperature of minus five degrees centigrade (23 degrees Fahrenheit), Absolut Icebar is literally the coolest place to hang out at in Tokyo. But guests need not freeze or pack winter coats. To prevent hypothermia, specially designed silver coloured ponchos and gloves are provided for each guest. Each stay is limited to 45 minutes to ensure a constant flow of guests, given the level of popularity it has enjoyed since its opening, and the fact that the maximum capacity is 50 people.

The ice used to create this frozen interior is imported all the way from North Sweden's Torne River. Even the ice "glasses" for the cocktails originate from the same river. The special purity of the water allows extraordinarily transparent ice block installations to be engraved with arctic flora and fauna graphics designed by Jens Thoms Ivarsson and Mats Nilsson. The complete icy interior of the bar changes twice a year, so guests may enjoy a refreshing experience on their next visit after a few months.

蒼き氷の世界にて、北の大地に生まれし美酒を味わう。

PHOTOGRAPHY	Ellen Nepilly
DESIGNER	Thoms & Nilsson
DESIGN TEAM	Jens Thoms Ivarsson, Mats Nilsson + Icehotel + Next Century Modern (graphic layout)
CONTRACTOR	Icehotel, V&S Absolut and Carrozzeria Japan
ADDRESS	4-2-4 The Wall, Nishiazabu, Minato-ku, Tokyo 150-0000
PHONE	+81 (0) 3 5464 2160
AREA	75 m²
SEATING	50 standing
COMPLETED	2006

大阪 ダンステリア サザエ

Danceteria Sazae

A whirl of entertainment all around

Sazae, which translates into "turban shell" in English, is not only the name of this club but also the theme of its design. The idea was to integrate the image of a shell's whorl into the interior. For designer Yoshiyuki Morii, it was particularly important to consider elements that are associated with a club - namely people, music, desire, or art, to name just a few - when creating the design.

Sazae's entrance area is very appealing, with a façade that reminds one of glittering black fish scales. After passing through the narrow entrance, one's anticipation grows with the pounding beat of the music, which gets louder with every step along a winding path to a spiral staircase leading up to the dance floor.

In contrast to the solid exterior, the interior is designed to awaken a feeling of soft comfort. Since the second and third levels are connected through a huge stairwell, Morii integrated slanted walls and attached crocodile panels for sound insulation. The panels not only reflect sound but also the dance floor's illumination, which can be adjusted to the beat of the music. Two counters to the right and left of the round dance floor put clubbers in the midst of the action even while drinking. With entertainment on four different floors, Sazae offers a space for everyone, with even a lounge where guests can relax next to a pool.

芸術と音楽が渦巻く、艶と粋が漂う、得も言われぬ空間。

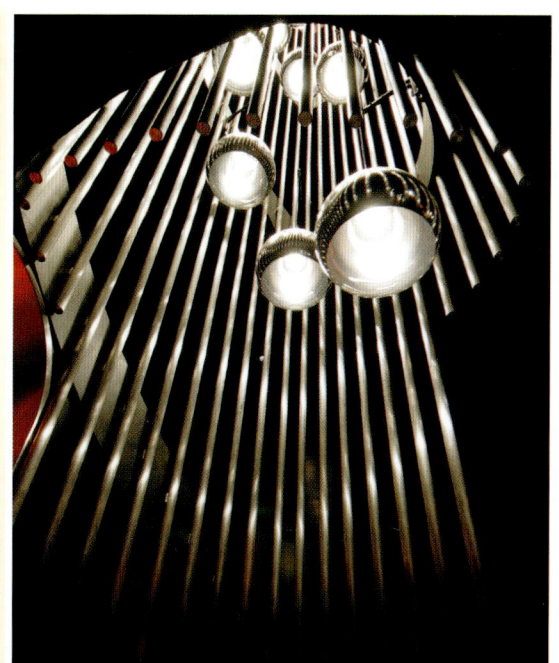

PHOTOGRAPHY	Shimomura Photo Office
DESIGNER	café co.
DESIGN TEAM	Yoshiyuki Morii
CONTRACTOR	Ing Styler, Inc.
ADDRESS	16-4 Chayamachi, Kita-ku, Osaka 530-0013
PHONE	+81 (0) 6 6486 3388
AREA	920 m²
SEATING	155 seats, 1 private room
COMPLETED	renewal open 2005

東京

北青山サロン

Kita Aoyama Salon
European underground

Located only one minute away from Kita Aoyama's Gaienmae station, this salon that is named after its location could not have been more conveniently situated. Kita Aoyama is the northern part of Aoyama, Tokyo's fashionable shopping district, which is famous not only for the flagship stores of many international brands but also the boutiques of leading Japanese designers.

Entering the door that leads to the staircase of Kita Aoyama Salon, guests may feel like they have just stepped into an old European wine cellar, with reminiscent sights and smells. The darkness may lend it a spooky feel initially, but upon arriving at the bottom of the staircase, huge lit candles welcome the visitors, and for a second, guests will forget that they are in Tokyo.

The interior is very dark and receive its only illumination from the candles, wall decorations, and the counter. Colourful insects in frames adorn one wall and creepy looking wooden African masks another. Most of the decoration and furniture are imported from antique shops or flea markets in Europe. Designer Takao Katsuta specially selected modern looking pieces on a trip to Europe and had them sent to Japan. The comfortable chairs at the counter were specially produced to fit Kita Aoyama Salon's interior. There is a private room where sexy photos in white frames adorn the walls. Small groups can comfortably sit on the floor, which is carpeted with leather mattresses and cushions – a cool place for small parties or groups.

忘れられた古城のような空間、人を内省に導く時間。

PHOTOGRAPHY	Ellen Nepilly
DESIGNER	LINE.Inc
DESIGN TEAM	Takao Katsuta
CONTRACTOR	Transit General Office, Inc.
ADDRESS	B1F, 2-7-18, Kita Aoyama, Minato-ku, Tokyo 107-0061
PHONE	+81 (0) 3 3479 7553
AREA	63 m²
SEATING	28 seats, 1 private room
COMPLETED	2007

茨城

リミックス

Remix

A contrast of passion and purity

Kyabakura is the abbreviated Japanese pronunciation for "cabaret club". It is very similar to the likes of hostess clubs except that the interior is not as exclusive, and therefore the charges are not as expensive. When designer Katsuya Iwamoto designed Remix, about six years had passed since he was first asked to design a kyabakura. At that time, some people were prejudiced against such places because they felt these clubs were not in accordance with Japanese customs. However, impressions have changed over the years. Now these clubs are widely accepted as hangouts where young people can go to drink and socialise in an informal, relaxed atmosphere.

Remix is conveniently situated only about two minutes away from Ibaraki station. Ibaraki is a suburban city of Osaka Prefecture, which is located between Osaka City and Kyoto. Since it is not a far commute to both metropolitan cities, the population in Ibaraki has been increasing steadily. Being a young and growing city, its inhabitants are a mix of people from widely different backgrounds. Thus Iwamoto's goal was to create an interior that demonstrates complementarity and contrast. He used the colours of red and white, balancing passion with purity. The stark contrast between both colours enhanced by the sharp lighting creates a pulsating atmosphere that suits the purpose of the space perfectly.

情熱と清潔感を色彩にした、ここは未来を語る社交場。

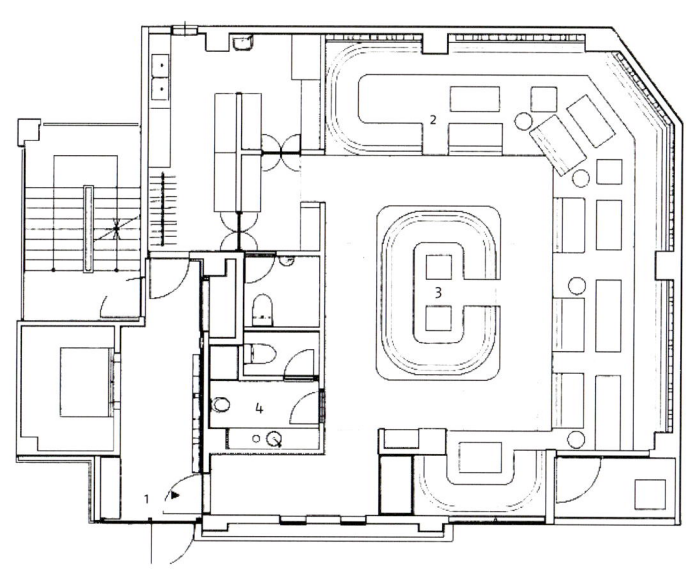

FLOORPLAN

1 entrance
2 lounging area
3 bar
4 washroom

PHOTOGRAPHY	Seiryo Yamada
DESIGNER	Embody Design Association
DESIGN TEAM	Katsuya Iwamoto
CONTRACTOR	Eternal Corporation
ADDRESS	2F, 2-27, Suehiro-cho, Ibaraki City, Osaka 567-0821
PHONE	+81 (0) 7 2630 0705
AREA	95 m²
COMPLETED	2006

東京

バース

Birth

A touch of Morocco

The light of a huge Moroccan lamp draws beautiful patterns on the wall at the entrance, inviting you to enter. Inside, candlelit tables, classic furniture with comfortable leather armchairs and couches, combined with a touch of Moroccan influence, create a cosy and relaxed ambience. Tranquil music and delicious cuisine - a fusion of Asian and French - make this bar an ideal place to spend some pleasant hours. Guests can even ask for a fortune-teller to come to their table and tell their future, certainly a privilege offered in very few bars.

Birth is also equipped with a soundproof karaoke room for VIPs, where a biometric fingerprint door lock keeps the unwanted out. Only friends of the owner and members can get in.

Designer Katsunori Suzuki was a big fan of the famous manga Hinotori (Phoenix) when he was young. He enlarged a double-page spread from the comic and attached it to a mirror in the karaoke room to give the space a special touch. Other visually arresting features include oil paintings of Moroccan-styled patterns in the main area, as well as several paintings of attractive long-haired women adorning the walls of the whole interior.

光の綾が出迎える空間で、時を忘れ、寛ぎに満たされる。

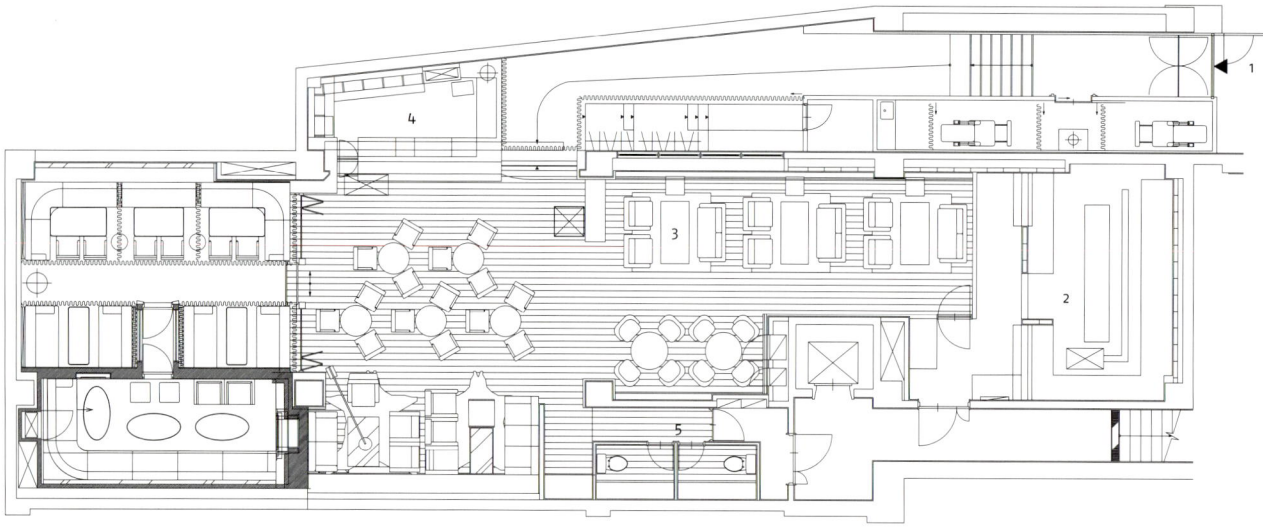

FLOORPLAN
1 entrance
2 kitchen
3 lounging area
4 bar
5 washroom

PHOTOGRAPHY	Masaya Yoshimura, Keisuke Miyamoto
DESIGNER	Fantastic Design Works
DESIGN TEAM	Katsunori Suzuki
CONTRACTOR	Birth Inc.
ADDRESS	B1F 2-24-12 Nishiazabu, Minato-ku, Tokyo 106-0031
PHONE	+81 (0) 3 3486 0330
AREA	295 m²
SEATING	68 seats
COMPLETED	2004

京都

ミネルバ

Minerva

Traditional grandeur lit with a modern touch

When designer Yukio Hashimoto was engaged to create a club out of this century-old house that belonged to the family of a former merchant, he visited the location to determine how to modernise it. When he first saw the traditional low threshold, the Juraku walls (a type of Japanese architecture characterised by yellowish-brown patterns, common in many Japanese tea rooms), and mirror-bedecked ceilings, Hashimoto was hesitant to remodel the house, because it would have meant destroying the beauty of its gorgeously balanced antique interior which had been maintained for so many years.

The building is located in Kyoto's old geisha district Gion, where many old houses remain and where the atmosphere of old Japan can still be felt. It would have been a shame to distort the house's character by modifying it halfheartedly. In order to preserve as much as possible of the interior, Hashimoto tapped the idea of utilising LED and fibre optics. The old space became a canvas on which he painted with dots of light. What makes this design so special is that it looks gorgeous during the night when the lights are on and when they are not, the interior reverts to its original appearance, with its distinctive essence intact.

Hashimoto is constantly pondering over ways to overcome the apparent incompatibility between tradition and new techniques. With this project, he has found one possible answer.

その煌めきは時代を超越し、粋人を魅了してやまない。

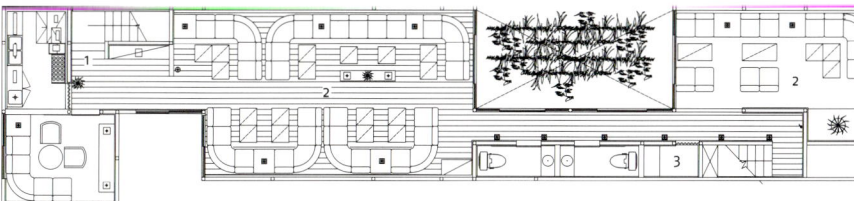

FIRST FLOOR

1 entrance
2 lounging area
3 washroom

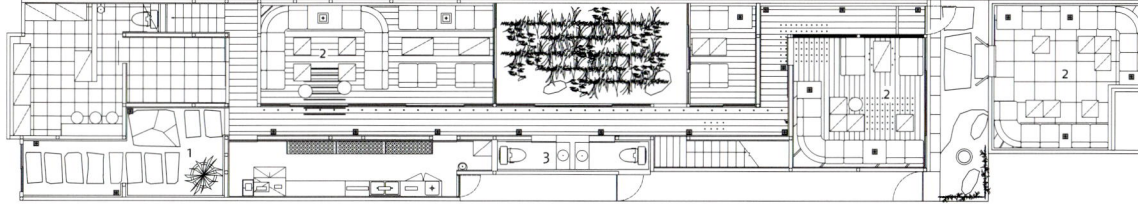

SECOND FLOOR

1 entrance
2 lounging area
3 washroom

PHOTOGRAPHY	Nakamichi Jun (Nacasa & Partners Inc.)
DESIGNER	Hashimoto Yukio Design Studio Inc.
DESIGN TEAM	Yukio Hashimoto, Shinichi Matsumoto
CONTRACTOR	Art Works Co., Ltd.
ADDRESS	106-4, Tominaga-cho, Yasaka Shinchi, Higashiyama-ku, Kyoto 605-0827
PHONE	+81 (0) 7 5532 3155
AREA	248 m²
SEATING	80 seats
COMPLETED	2004

千葉

七蔵

Shichi-Zo
Mythological beasts coming to life in ink

Due to the quick growth of the Tokyo area in the 1960s, Matsudo City, where Shichi-Zo is sited, developed into a large commuter town. The city is located in Chiba, a prefecture next to Tokyo on the Pacific coast.

When owner Takao Yuasa met with designer Taro Maeda, he asked him to create a simple interior that would also possess captivating originality. During the conversation, Yuasa spoke of pride in his family name, Shichi-Zo, because it is a "yago" name, an exclusive honour that common people used to denote their distinctive identities during feudal times. At that time, family names were typically still the privilege of the upper class, such as the samurai families, while most commoners were simply named after the houses they lived in.

Fascinated and inspired by this distinctive traditional Japanese characteristic, Maeda suggested naming the bar Shichi-Zo and adding a touch of traditional Japanese style to the design. Drawing from designs with a similar individuality, such as manga (Japanese comics), Maeda came up with the idea to use irezumi for the counter. Maeda applied irezumi, which literally means "insert ink", a form of Japanese tattoo-based art, to illustrate mythological creatures in black ink that transformed the countertop into an eye-catching tableau. The pillars and shelves behind the counter were painted crimson red, offering a felicitous contrast to the strong impact of the black ink and rounding up this well-balanced interior.

龍躍る卓上で杯を交わし、重ね、内なる龍を制する夜。

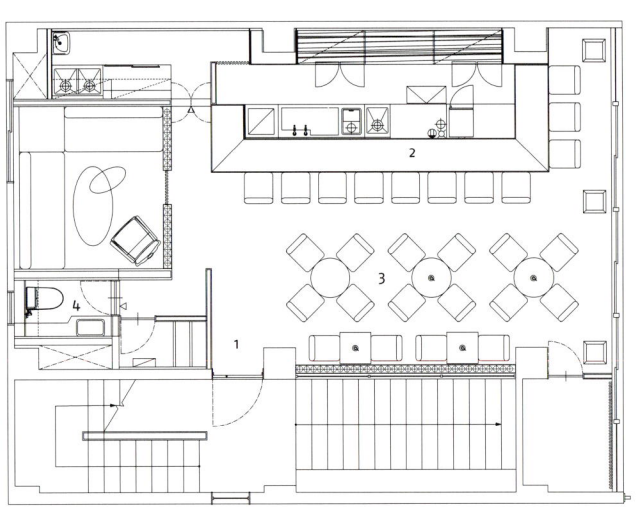

FLOORPLAN
1 entrance
2 bar
3 lounging area
4 washroom

PHOTOGRAPHY	Hiroshi Tsujitani (Nacasa & Partners Inc.)
DESIGNER	Bayleaf Inc. & Descartes Inc.
DESIGN TEAM	Taro Maeda, Takumi Sato
CONTRACTOR	Takao Yuasa
ADDRESS	2F Machi Bldg., 177 Matsudo, Matsudo City, Chiba 271-0092
PHONE	+81 (0) 4 7366 6636
AREA	65 m²
SEATING	35 seats
COMPLETED	2006

東京 ザズル

Zazzle

Accommodating privacy seekers and limelight chasers

A short walk away from Tokyo's nightlife hotspot Roppongi, the more quiet and relaxed Nishiazabu area offers a wide selection of fashionable bars, restaurants and clubs. Zazzle is one of its highlights. Located near the well-known Nishi Azabu crossing, but hidden in a quiet side road, Zazzle is frequented mostly by regular customers. Hence the friendly atmosphere is much more relaxed, when compared to other nearby establishments crowded with heavy human traffic.

Interestingly, this eclectic interior has two counters: one stands at the rear of the room, before a distinctive wall that is partly wood and partly a red illumination panel, while the other is located on the left. On the left side of the room, the wall is panelled with white illuminated marble, making the polished bright red counter in front of it shine even more. The counter's legs are made of clear acrylic with enclosed bubbles, and the diagonally braced construction creates an interesting effect. People who like to be seen might prefer sitting in the illumination of the latter, while those who prefer to people-watch gather at the other less conspicuous counter filled with red subdued light.

The area in the centre of the room looks as if square cushions of various colours were piled like bricks and flagstones above each other to create partition walls, seats and tables. However, they can be moved and rearranged to suit the number of guests in a group. There are also two other private karaoke rooms that can be booked.

緋色が綾なす時間、和らぎが包む空間がやすらぎを生む。

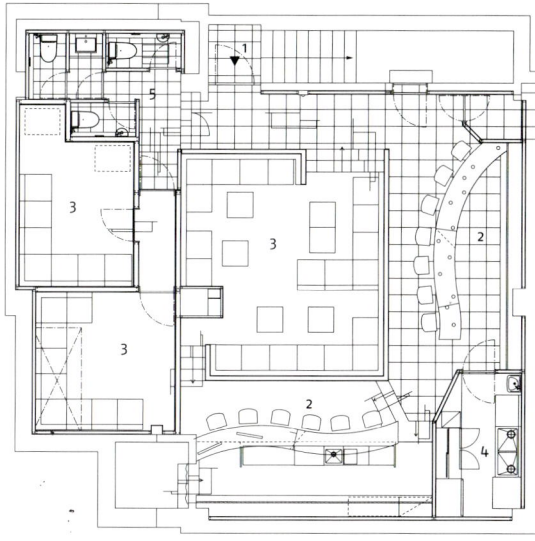

FLOORPLAN

1 entrance
2 bar
3 lounging area
4 kitchen
5 washroom

PHOTOGRAPHY	Ellen Nepilly
DESIGNER	Prostyle Design Co., ltd
DESIGN TEAM	Tetsuya Hamana
CONTRACTOR	Jun Suzuki, Yutaka Taguchi
ADDRESS	3-17-20 B1F Nishiazabu, Minato-ku, Tokyo 106-0031
PHONE	+81 (0) 3 3796 7207
AREA	142 m²
SEATING	48 seats, 2 private rooms
COMPLETED	2006

東京

志村や

Shimuraya

A return to tradition with sugi wood

In old Japan, large amounts of sugi (commonly known as Japanese cedar, but really more a type of cypress) wood were specially used for building temples and houses. The enormous monoculture that accompanied the large-scale reforesting of sugi trees, and the declining demand since then, is causing enormous problems for the Japanese ecosystem today. The Japanese population also suffers from an increase in allergies to the excessive amount of sugi tree pollen.

Koji Shimura became increasingly interested in the topic of sugi and joined a club of people who believe that the use of sugi as a raw material in Japan must be encouraged once more. So when Shimura decided to open his own bar, it was natural for him to use sugi wood for the interior. He approached architect Shigemasa Noi, who is known for his sublime use of natural wood for interiors. The result is this gorgeous standing bar, named after its owner.

Shimuraya's interior is made entirely of natural, untreated wood - only the floor is oiled to make it more resistant. Inside, the woody scent and the relaxing atmosphere only an organic material can produce, combine to create a feeling of being in a natural oasis in Tokyo's concrete city jungle. The ambience alone is so cosy that many guests stay for a long time, even though there are no seats.

木に包まれる空間で木が躍動する、それは温もりのある場。

PHOTOGRAPHY	Ellen Nepilly
DESIGNER	Shigemasa Noi Design Office
DESIGN TEAM	Shigemasa Noi, Yuki Masuda
CONTRACTOR	Office Two Platon
ADDRESS	Nihonbashi, Ningyo-cho 2-20-7, Chuo-ku, Tokyo 103-0013
PHONE	+81 (0) 3 5652 1145
AREA	20 m²
SEATING	18 standing
COMPLETED	2006

東京

アメーバー

Amebar

Elegance in a quiet space

Dogenzaka is the name of a hill in Shibuya, the hippest and most vibrant of Tokyo's 23 districts. Shibuya is a gathering spot for the young and is the centre of Japanese youth culture - but it has much more to offer. The streets of Dogenzaka are known to host a large selection of love hotels, but there are also chic and upscale restaurants and bars in the area, with Amebar heading the list. Built by the CEO of one of the biggest Internet media companies in Japan, this establishment is a private bar, although non-members may still be admitted.

Amebar is located on the third floor of a building that looks like a regular apartment house from the street. Time seems to slow down when one exits the elevator and walks through the entrance into the calmness of the interior. The simple but elegant space and subdued lighting make this atmosphere very cosy and tranquil.

The walls are made of tinted black clinker, the floor and counter created from reddish warm wood, while heavy dark turquoise curtains keep out glaring neon lights from outside. Comfortable armchairs are placed on an elevated platform lit on both sides, so that guests need not sit uncomfortably on bar stools. The shelf for the bottles is one of the few sources of light in the room, and is illuminated from below, which nicely accentuates the counter area. By combining this with the flames of the oil lamps that seem to float in the air, as well as the light from the raised seating platform, designer Katsunori Suzuki creates lovely visual effects.

褐色の輝きが、この上ない落ち着きと大人の香を醸し出す。

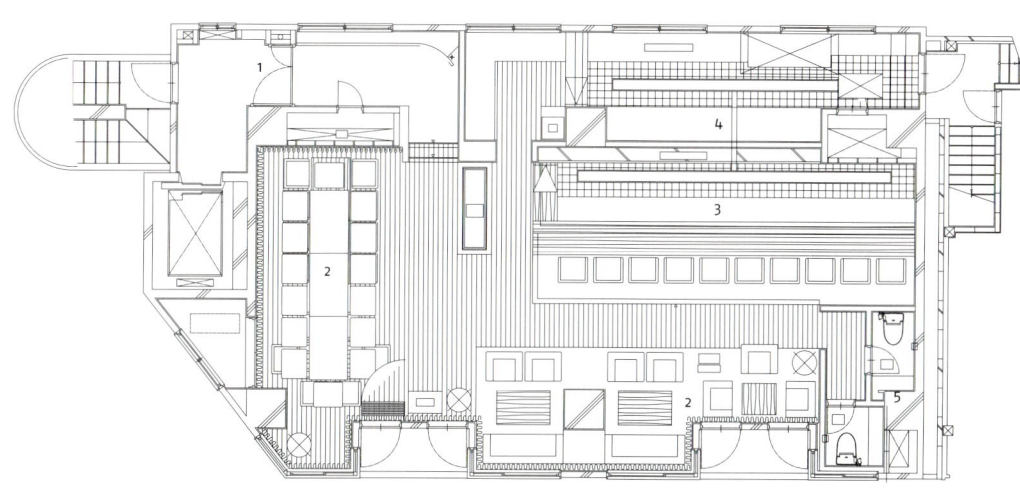

FLOORPLAN
1. entrance
2. lounging area
3. bar
4. kitchen
5. washroom

PHOTOGRAPHY	Masaya Yoshimura (Nacasa & Partners Inc.)
DESIGNER	Fantastic Design Works
DESIGN TEAM	Katsunori Suzuki
CONTRACTOR	Start works Inc.
ADDRESS	Dogenzaka Plaza Nishinaya Building 3F, 1-18-8, Dogenzaka, Shibuya-ku, Tokyo 150-0043
PHONE	+81 (0) 3 3770 0750
AREA	134 m²
SEATING	34 seats
COMPLETED	2005

大阪

ライブ アンド バー オンジェム

Live & Bar 11

Jamming with the house band any way you like

With more than 800 sqm of floor space, the area of Live & Bar 11 is huge. Divided into three large and distinct sections, the establishment offers guests different themes to choose from, and allows them to enjoy the evening according to their taste. Starting with the heart of the live house, which is composed of a round interior that includes a concert hall and a stage, spectators can sit comfortably on classic leather chairs to watch the performing band. Different events are held almost every day, ranging from Tango Argentina shows to jazz concerts.

On the left to the front of the house is a small round room separated from the main hall. It includes a stylish circular counter with an illuminated top that somehow reminds one of a beach bar. Guests can enjoy cocktails around the counter, while still enjoying the best possible view of the stage that a separate room offers, and listen to the music undisturbed.

If the performing band does not suit the taste of some, they can opt to relax in the VIP lounge to the right of the house, where an extra fee is charged by the hour, or take the less expensive party rooms to the left. The concept of Live & Bar 11 is based upon the style of old Parisian cabarets. Designer Yoshiyuki Morii's use of wine-red colours for the curtains and decorations, combined with classic furniture and chandeliers, establishes an atmosphere with just the right touch of exclusivity.

極上の赤と輝く白、華麗で優美で大胆な夜を楽しむ。

PHOTOGRAPHY	Shimomura Photo Office
DESIGNER	café co.
DESIGN TEAM	Yoshiyuki Morii
CONTRACTOR	Ing Styler, Inc.
ADDRESS	Midosuji Bldg. 11F 1-4-5 Nishi-Shinsaibashi, Chuo-ku, Osaka 542-0086
PHONE	+81 (0) 6 6243 0089
AREA	827 m²
SEATING	160 seats, 4 private rooms
COMPLETED	2006

大阪

ゾディアック

Zodiac

Astrology signs light the way in this girls bar

In this Osaka bar named Zodiac, only females may serve as bartenders. Zodiac is one of the so-called "garuzu ba", which is Japanese for "girls' bar". Contrary to what the name might suggest, these bars are neither strip clubs nor hang outs for lesbians. The main purpose of "garuzu ba" is to entertain male customers, but they do not exclude female customers from having a drink there as well. Such bars have been around for many decades in Japan, but the tag is relatively new and has only just become increasingly popular.

Girls working in "garuzu ba" mix drinks and entertain the customers. However, they remain behind the counter and do not sit with customers as hostesses would. Furthermore, the cost of drinks and other charges in "garuzu ba" is usually not much higher than those of regular bars, so there is hardly any point of comparison with hostess clubs. The draw of "garuzu ba" lies in the cute factor of the staff, much like the ladies of Coyote Ugly made famous by Jerry Bruckheimer.

Zodiac's furniture and interior is kept simple, so the graphics on the ceiling become even more captivating in contrast. As the bar's name might suggest, these graphics are actually depictions of the twelve astrological constellations. On first sight, they appear to be luminous, but these are actually just reflections. The tabletops below them are mirrors covered with an opaque foil that has reflective cutouts in the form of these graphics. When light is shone upon them, these graphics are reflected against the ceiling. Designer Masaru Shimizu explained that it was very difficult finding right angular adjustments to achieve this amazing effect.

十二宮が光り輝き、清廉で魅惑的なひとときが生まれる。

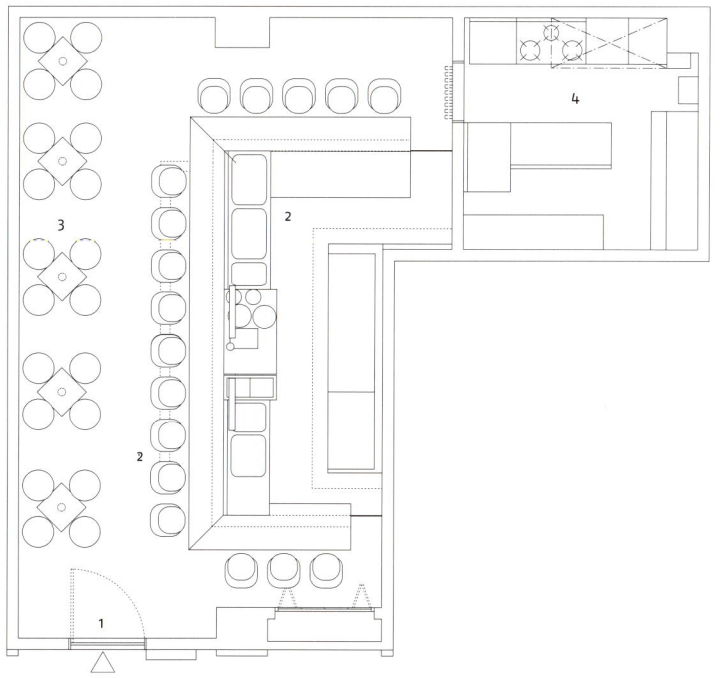

FLOORPLAN

1 entrance
2 bar
3 lounging area
4 kitchen

PHOTOGRAPHY	Yoshihisa Araki
DESIGNER	Space Planning-LAR
DESIGN TEAM	Masaru Shimizu
CONTRACTOR	Theory Factory Co., Ltd.
ADDRESS	Kitanaka Bldg. 3F, 8-13-3 Nishinaka-Jima, Yodogawa-ku, Osaka 532-0011
PHONE	+81 (0) 6 6101 0090
AREA	49 m²
SEATING	37 seats
COMPLETED	2006

大阪　ル キャバレ

Le Cabaret

Seeking cosy warmth down the copper tunnel

Since the use of industrially manufactured goods is widespread in Japan, architect Tadashi Suga's idea for this Osaka bar was to create something with a less industrialised feel. The entrance of Le Cabaret is stunning, with a 3.6 m-deep copper tunnel integrated into the façade of the building. All passersby cannot help but be attracted by it, giving this unique entrance an enticing effect indeed.

Huge Japanese cities like Tokyo and Osaka where concrete buildings prevail have less of an Old World charm when compared to many European cities. Entering Le Cabaret through the copper tunnel makes guests feel as if they are stepping into another country. While the interior reminds guests of a Spanish tapas bar, and the atmosphere has an European feel to it, it is not just a Western copy. The bar has its own special individuality. A long solid, curved counter in the front area and a hanging illumination offer visual distractions. Although the space is rectangular, the interior seems smaller and hence feels cosier.

Whereas guests have to stand at the tables in the front, the room at the back of the bar has comfortable seats for relaxation. The homely atmosphere created by the warm colours of the furniture, the stonewall and the wooden floor is further amplified when the bartender turns on the fireplace. Guests can sit with a glass of wine, watch the crackling flames, and enjoy the feeling of being on holiday in a faraway country.

落ち着いた輝き、そして品格のある赤が生む華やぎ。

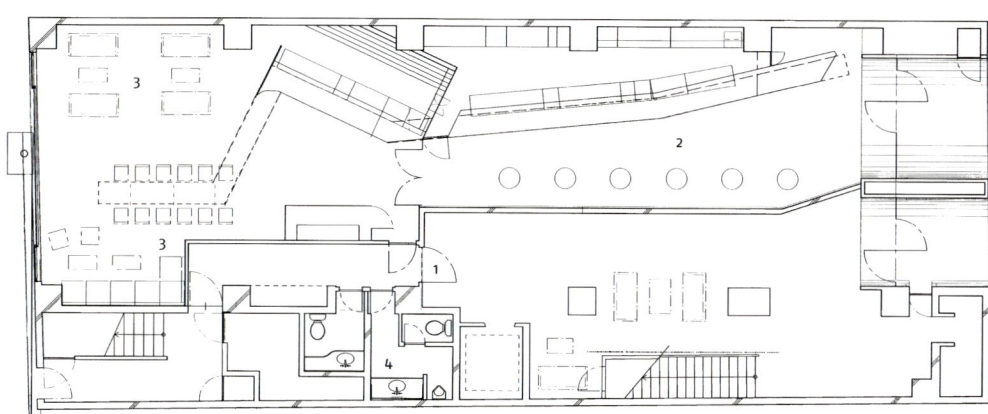

FLOORPLAN

1 entrance
2 bar
3 lounging area
4 washroom

PHOTOGRAPHY	Ellen Nepilly
DESIGNER	Suga Architects Office co., ltd.
DESIGN TEAM	Tadashi Suga
CONTRACTOR	Vert Trust
ADDRESS	4-5-4 Honmachi, Chuo-Ku, Osaka 541-0053
PHONE	+81 (0) 6 6265 8201
AREA	159 m²
SEATING	30 seats, 40 standing
COMPLETED	2005

Club Zoo

Fun on the wild side

As you might have guessed, the theme of this club is based on animal motifs, which have been used throughout its exclusive interior. Stuffed animal heads adorn the walls while mosaic serpent skin patterns decorate part of the floor and the restrooms. Guests can occupy the black leather seats located below hanging deer heads at the entrance area while waiting for admission.

An American fashion photographer's gorgeous photographs encased in rococo-style frames help enhance the walls of the main area. Designer Hiroyuki Matsunaka created this dazzling picture by enhancing an outstanding photograph of a sexy blonde model with the image of a beautiful butterfly. Arranged on snake patterns, it is wonderfully eye-catching. Matsunaka virtually designed the entire interior on his own, including the cushions that decorate some of the couches.

Club Zoo is one of many hostess clubs in Japan. They are different from clubs where people go to dance, but they are still considered "clubs". Men go there to have drinks, to sit and chat with the girls who work there. Usually, women are also admitted. These clubs are part of Japan's business culture, and companies may invite potential customers to such establishments to build crucial corporate relationships. Hostesses basically fulfill a role similar to that of the traditional geishas – they are still entertainers, albeit on a different level. There are many variations of such clubs, but Club Zoo is definitely one of the more exclusive ones.

時を超え空間を超え、日常を忘れ、明日を考えぬ。

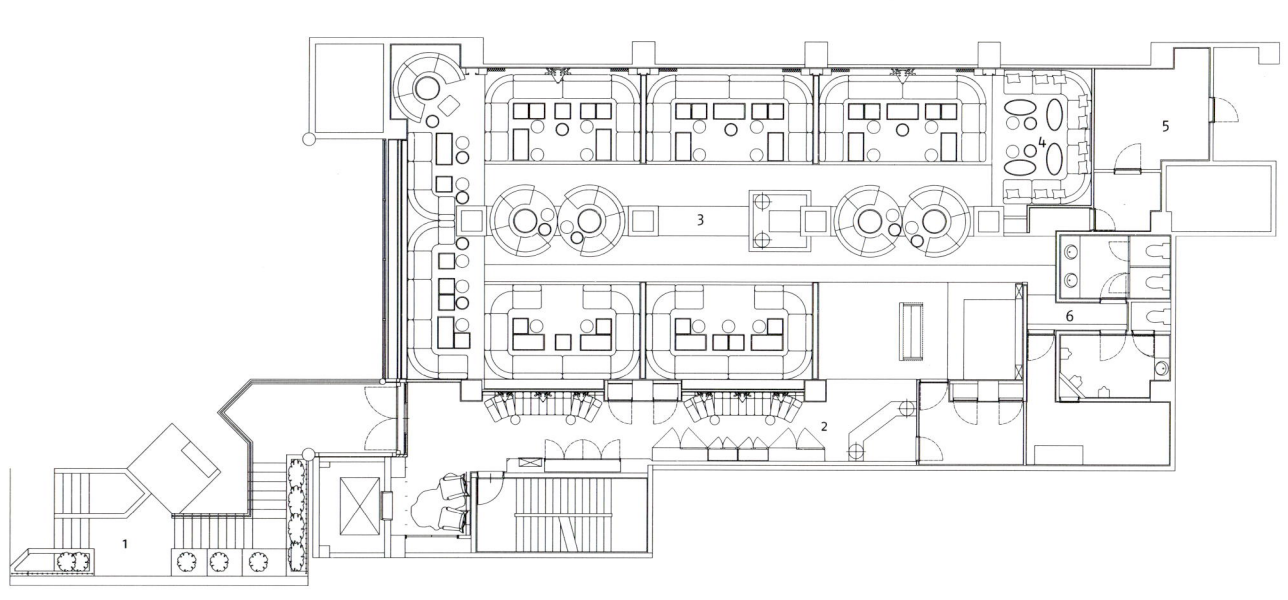

FLOORPLAN

1. entrance
2. reception
3. lounging area
4. VIP lounge
5. staff room
6. washroom

PHOTOGRAPHY	Yoshihisa Araki
DESIGNER	design room 702
DESIGN TEAM	Hiroyuki Matsunaka
ADDRESS	Shibaraku Building 2F, 2-7-18 Higashi-Shinsaibashi, Chuo-ku, Osaka 542-0083
PHONE	+81 (0) 6 6212 1258
AREA	328 m²
SEATING	140 seats
COMPLETED	2005

西宮

ユーロカフェ

Euro Café
Interior comfort, exterior beauty

This trattoria bar sits in a quiet neighbourhood in Nishinomiya, a city of Hyogo Prefecture situated between Osaka and Kobe. Due to the proximity of the Kobe port, the Kansai region has a long history of western influence. As a result, many western-style buildings are still present. Shukugawa church, which is located opposite Euro Café, is one of them. Although it was built in the 1930s, its gorgeous architecture reminds one of old European Gothic churches. To celebrate this lovely location, designer Katsuya Iwamoto designed Euro Café so that guests can enjoy this beautiful sight.

Iwamoto designed a curved exterior wall for Euro Café and integrated huge sliding windows that can be opened on warm days. He also positioned a large bench just by the windows that sits both guests on the inside and outside of the bar, hence unifying the interior space with the exterior. The goal was to create a design that betters the connection between the people, the space and the city. Euro Café's warm and friendly atmosphere with its European influence thus blends perfectly with the surrounding.

一歩踏み込むとそこは異文化、欧州の街角を彷徨う楽しみ。

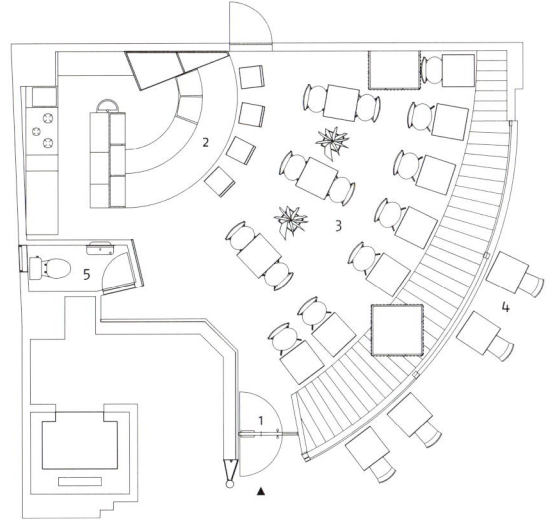

FLOORPLAN
1 entrance
2 bar
3 lounging area
4 outdoor terrace
5 washroom

PHOTOGRAPHY	Seiryo Yamada
DESIGNER	Embody Design Association
DESIGN TEAM	Katsuya Iwamoto
CONTRACTOR	projéct works inc.
ADDRESS	1F 5-12, Hagoromo-cho, Nishinomiya City, Hyogo 662-0051
PHONE	+81 (0) 7 9822 3366
AREA	76 m²
SEATING	30 seats
COMPLETED	2003

金沢

ロッサ

Rosa

A modern form of traditional hospitality

Kanazawa, the capital city of Ishikawa Prefecture, is located along the Sea of Japan and borders the Japan Alps. After Kyoto, it is Japan's second largest city that was not destroyed during the Second World War. Hence, parts of the old castle town are still in good condition. During the feudal period, there was a custom known as "oyobare" in Kanazawa. To help visitors find their way, lights were put on stepping stones in the garden to show special hospitality.

Following this beautiful tradition, designer Katsuya Iwamoto integrated round lights and rose petals into the floor. These outstanding lights lead guests on their way from the entrance to the seating area inside Rosa. It was important for Iwamoto to include Kanazawa's distinctive culture and traditions in the modern design of Rosa. With the lights in the floor, he created a modern form of "oyobare".

Furthermore, he felt that the atmosphere of the space should not only create a relaxing vibe but also involve some feeling of activity. For a hostess club, where the goal is to encourage conversation, the use of a lucent red colour produces just the right ambience.

薔薇色の時空間に包まれ、今宵、万感の思いを語る。

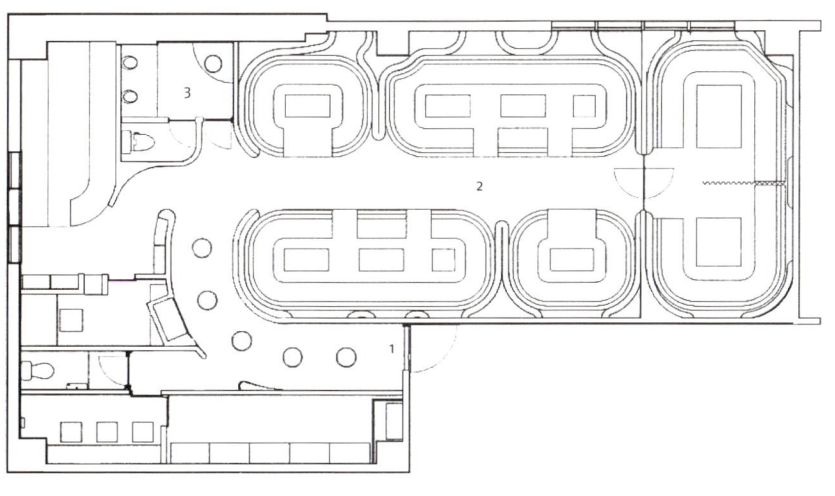

FLOORPLAN

1. entrance
2. lounging area
3. washroom

PHOTOGRAPHY	Seiryo Yamada
DESIGNER	Katsuya Iwamoto
DESIGN TEAM	Katsuya Iwamoto + Embody Design Association
CONTRACTOR	Art Works Co., Ltd.
ADDRESS	7F, 3-111, Horikawa-cho, Kanazawa City, Ishikawa 920-0847
PHONE	+81 (0) 7 6223 2100
AREA	148 m²
COMPLETED	2004

横浜 シーサイド

Seaside

A water fountain shooting for the heavens

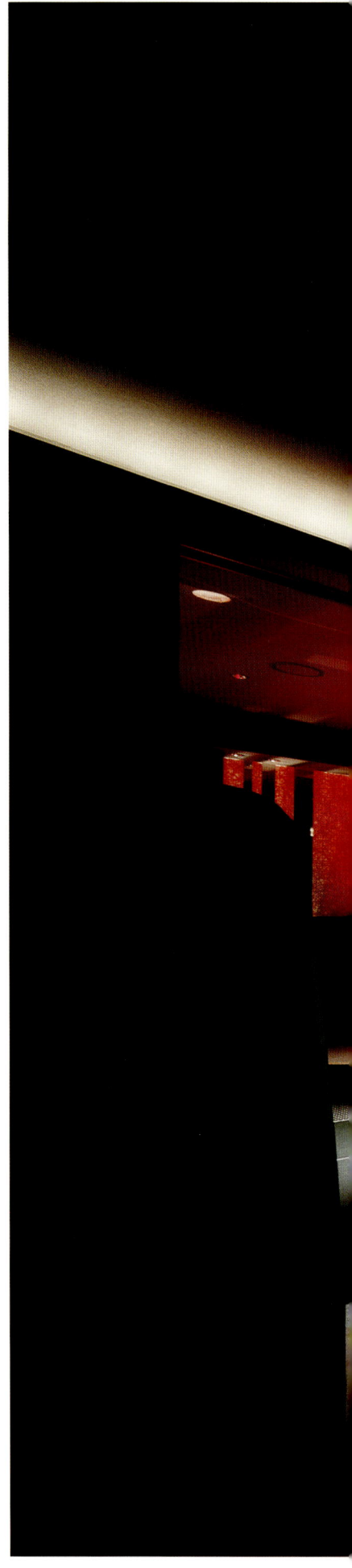

Located in the heart of bustling quarters just three minutes by foot from Yokohama station, this "kyabakura" club is easily accessible. The area's close proximity to the Pacific Ocean gave Seaside its name, and water became the theme for the interior. Typical guests include sophisticated adults who want to spend a cheerful evening in a relaxed atmosphere. Japanese businessmen who want to forget the stress of the day and make easy conversation with good-looking girls often seek to spend some time in clubs like Seaside before returning home.

The interior's main setting is calm, with dark furniture and low-key lighting. This calmness accentuates a dramatic illuminating visual effect – a towering blue column made of mosaic tiles standing in the heart of the establishment, resembling a fountain of water shooting into the sky. This image is made all the more realistic through the use of gradient colours – a lighter blue on the bottom and a darker blue at the top.

For the VIP room, designer Akitoshi Imafuku wanted to create something different. He created walls with patterns of complex curves in different sizes crossing and intersecting each other to create the impression of water bubbles. Contrary to the typical association of water with the colour blue, he used red to create an exceptional visual effect.

光り輝く泡沫、天空に駆ける水流に魅せられる空間。

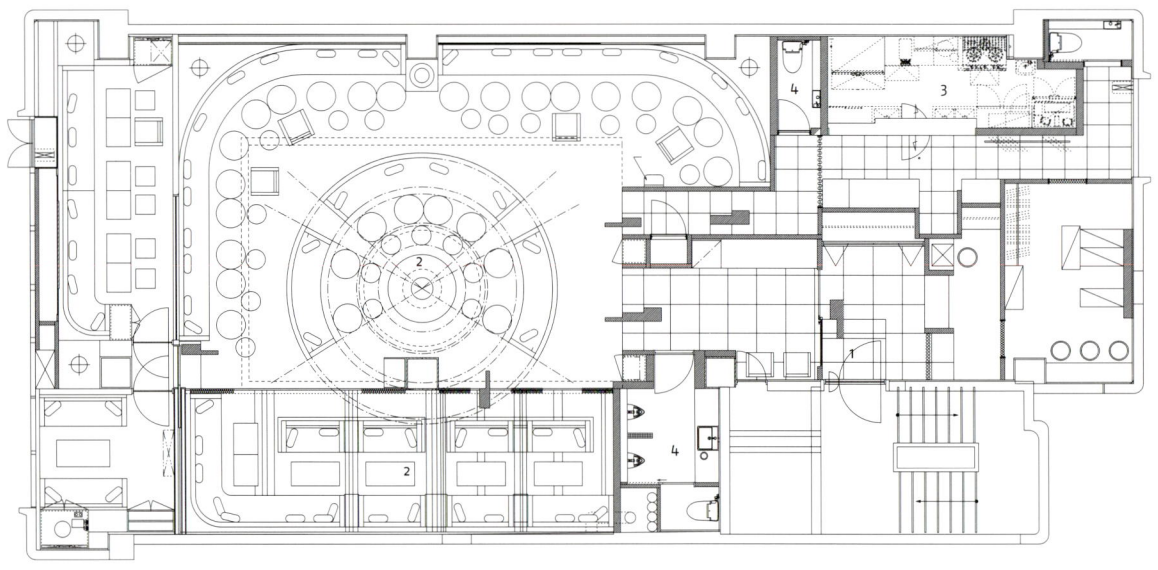

FLOORPLAN
1 entrance
2 lounging area
3 kitchen
4 washroom

PHOTOGRAPHY	Yoshihisa Araki
DESIGNER	Supermaniac Inc.
DESIGN TEAM	Akitoshi Imafuku
CONTRACTOR	Prince Corporation
ADDRESS	3F 1-12-9 Minami-Saiwai, Nishi-ku, Yokohama City, Kanagawa 220-0005
PHONE	+81 (0) 4 5311 7087
AREA	207 m^2
SEATING	46 seats
COMPLETED	2006

西宮
酒蔵路

Sakuraji
The hanging Japanese Zen rock gardens

Japanese Zen rock gardens form the foundation for Sakuraji's design theme. Designer Yusaku Kaneshiro and his team created them artificially by applying forms in acrylic on panels. Mounted over the counters, some distance from the ceiling, the gardens seem to float in midair. The ceiling is clad with mirrors reflecting the whole floorscene below it. The reflected rock gardens create a stunning effect. Kaneshiro also used mirrors on parts of the walls to visually enlarge Sakuraji's small interior.

The stunted tree and real rocks, combined with illuminated white acrylic rocks on sand arranged in one corner of the room, resemble the remains from the stage set for a fantasy film. A huge illuminated panel depicts the four seasons, forming a beautiful piece of art. Mounted behind a counter in two parts, it is eye-catching enough to stop not just visitors, but even passersby on the street.

The interior offers another interesting feature: the many sugidama (cedar balls) hanging from the ceiling. These are traditional Japanese decorations made of sugi (Japanese cedar) tree needles, and measure approximately 20 cm in diameter. Sake brewers usually hang one in front of their brewery as a sign showing that sake is available for sale. According to Kaneshiro, it was no mean feat to get so many sugidama for the interior.

天地左右境界の無い空間で、籠を外す、羽根を休める。

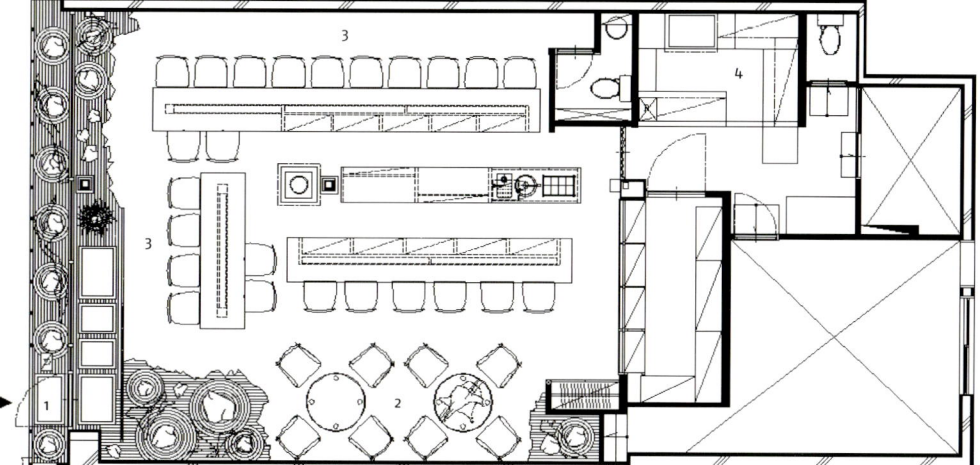

FLOORPLAN
1 entrance
2 lounging area
3 bar
4 washroom

PHOTOGRAPHY	Masahiro Ishibashi
DESIGNER	Zoukei Syudan Co., Ltd.
DESIGN TEAM	Yusaku Kaneshiro, Mitsuru Komatsuzaki
CONTRACTOR	Hujioka
ADDRESS	5-7-12 Naruo-cho, Nishinomiya City, Hyogo 663-8184
PHONE	+81 (0) 7 9847 2007
AREA	33 m²
SEATING	32 seats
COMPLETED	2006

大阪

B bar Umeda

Exclusive French crystal extravagance

Definitely one of Osaka's most exclusive bars, B bar showcases French crystal at its finest. Baccarat, a crystal manufacturer with 243 years of history, owns three bars in the world - B bar Umeda being its latest venture.

Opulent design is amplified by red leather stools and seats, a 12 m-long counter made from a single piece of wood, and a 24-light black Zenith chandelier. These create the perfect atmosphere for a special night out. The ambience of the interior accentuates a more than 300 Baccarat crystal glasses on the wall around the lounge area, which crystal fans would be delighted to explore. Bottles and glasses used to serve drinks are all stowed away in cupboards integrated in the design so that, unlike in other bars, the area around the counter always looks neat.

To serve the drinks, the bartender specially selects one of the exquisite glasses - all shaped and engraved differently - for each guest. Customers may also request a special glass to their liking. There is also a humidor where an exclusive cigar selection is offered. Even the coasters are specially designed for B bar and are a testament the bar's acute attention to detail. In the restroom, guests will find historical Baccarat crystal perfume bottles from a museum in France.

豪華でなく上質、華美ではなく優美。艶のある空間。

PHOTOGRAPHY	Baccarat Pacific K.K.
DESIGNER	Kimiaki Takahashi
DESIGN TEAM	Kimiaki Takahashi
CONTRACTOR	Baccarat Pacific K.K.
ADDRESS	Hilton Plaza East 2F, 1-8-16, Umeda, Kita-ku, Osaka 530-0001
PHONE	+81 (0) 6 6341 2375
AREA	135 m²
SEATING	40 seats
COMPLETED	2005

京都 エスタジ

Estasi

A leopard grinning from the wall

This lounge bar is set in Kyoto's famous Gion district. Since the city was not reduced to rubble like most of the other Japanese cities during the Second World War, entire streets of old traditional buildings have been preserved up until now. Estasi's main entrance is equipped with the lovely wooden sliding doors that are characteristic of the townscape of Gion.

Upon entering these doors, guests find themselves in an amazing corridor with chandeliers and crystal chains adorning the wall to the right. The other wall is clad with mirrors that reflect this splendid image, which makes the room seem much more spacious. At the end of the hall, an automatic door leads visitors into the lounge area. The VIP rooms are located past the long counter equipped with comfortable leatherette stools. The first of the rooms functions as a cigar lounge, where the main visual feature is that of a huge red grinning leopard on the wall. The fantastic illustration is painted with red and green and looks great together with the crimson red couches in the room. Amazingly, the bookshelf by the wall is a hidden door to another VIP space, a karaoke and party room. The felicitous blend of the modern and the classic makes Estasi the perfect choice for a tasteful evening in Gion.

ここは典雅の世界、時代を超えた美意識が息吹く場所。

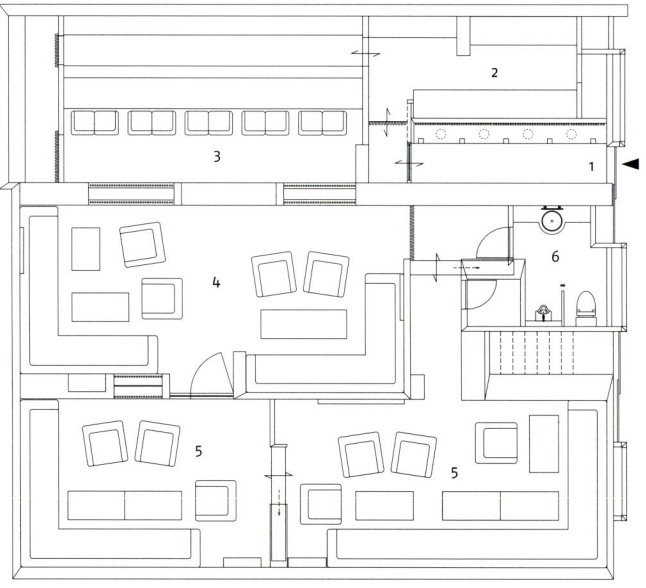

FLOORPLAN
1 entrance
2 kitchen
3 bar
4 lounging area
5 VIP lounge
6 washroom

PHOTOGRAPHY	Hirokazu Matsuoka
DESIGNER	Kis Design Associates
DESIGN TEAM	Atsushi Korekane, Yoko Nagai, Hiromi Nakai, Sayuri Moriwaki
CONTRACTOR	Yoji Akamatsu
ADDRESS	347-91 Gionmachi, Kitagawa Higashiyama-ku, Kyoto 605-0073
PHONE	+81 (0) 7 5541 0648
AREA	150 m²
SEATING	35 seats, 2 private rooms
COMPLETED	2006

東京

クラブ ビゼ

Club Bisser

A bloom of erotic flowers and crystal sprays

Ginza, Tokyo's most upmarket area, is an appropriate location for Club Bisser. This hostess club is certainly the most exclusive one in Tokyo, and possibly even in all of Japan. The Baccarat chandelier that forms the core of the establishment alone is worth the price of a sports car.

Every single part of this interior is painstakingly thought out and could hardly be more exclusive. The club's interior design is a fusion of the classic and the modern, conceptualised entirely by designer Hiroyuki Matsunaka, right down to the furniture and even the relief on some of the pieces. He based the furniture design on a traditional European style from the Middle Ages – the classic element – and combined it with different modern elements such as modern photographs, since art also plays an important role in Matsunaka's design.

Famous Japanese photographer Nobuyoshi Araki's photographs of erotic flowers adorn the main area and VIP rooms, adding a special touch to the scene. Mosaics of tens of thousands of Swarovski crystals clad part of the walls in the private rooms and the hallway – clearly a Herculean task for the craftsmen, but the effect is stunning.

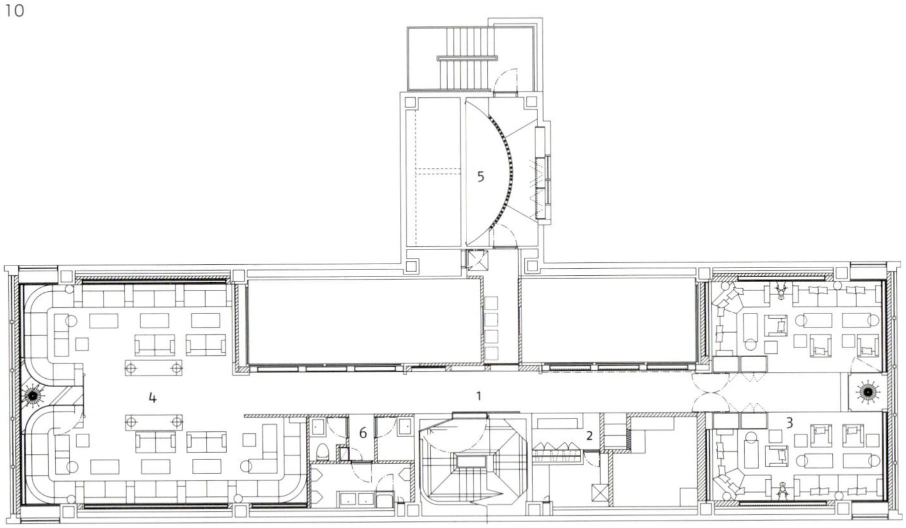

FLOORPLAN

1. entrance
2. reception
3. VIP lounge
4. lounging area
5. staff room
6. washroom

寛ぎと緊張が空間を二分する、隙のない自分を演出する世界。

PHOTOGRAPHY	Takeshi Nakasa (Nacasa & Partners Inc.)
DESIGNER	design room 702
DESIGN TEAM	Hiroyuki Matsunaka
ADDRESS	Water Bldg. 2F, 8-6-2 Ginza, Chuo-Ku, Tokyo 104-0061
PHONE	+81 (0) 3 3569 0607
AREA	245 m²
SEATING	58 seats
COMPLETED	2006

大阪

ル サンク

Le Cinq

Bar lounge à la Paris

This elegant bar lounge is located just off Osaka's major district and shopping area Shinsaibashi. Designed after Parisian lounges, the charming interior and its grand selection of French wines make this upscale establishment a great location for a relaxed night out.

With its subdued lighting and a ceiling richly covered with leaves, the staircase leading down to the basement, where Le Cinq sits, is already a fascinating sight. In the main room, the captivating mirrored wall, the stonewalls, and the exceptional wall that continues to be decorated with rich green leaves all skillfully blend with the classic furnishing and counter area.

In the VIP room, the vintage black-and-white photographs in golden frames and the huge black retro leather couch and chairs standing before European-styled retro wallpaper combine to create an appealing ambience. Le Cinq certainly lives up to its motto "bon chic bon sens," which effectively means "good looking and chic" and is derived from the French expression "bon chic bon genre."

質実剛健。上質な空間で、上質な酒を飾らず楽しむために。

PHOTOGRAPHY	Takeshi Nakasa (Nacasa & Partners Inc.)
DESIGNER	design room 702
DESIGN TEAM	Hiroyuki Matsunaka
CONTRACTOR	Eiichi Kunitomo
ADDRESS	Unagidani Block B1, 1-19-15 Higashi-Shinsaibashi, Chuo-Ku, Osaka 542-0083
PHONE	+81 (0) 6 6245 6115
AREA	102 m²
SEATING	33 seats
COMPLETED	2007

徳島

りゅくすバーいーつ

Luxe Bar Eats

An appreciation of Japanese Wabi-sabi

Luxe Bar Eats is located in Tokushima city, a town on Shikoku Island, the smallest of the four Japanese main islands. Compared with huge metropolises like Osaka and Tokyo, Tokushima, with its 260,000 inhabitants, is incredibly tiny. Even though there are quite a few bars and restaurants in the district of Akita-machi, the selection of fashionable places to hang out at is very limited. Bar owner Tadashi Yonezawa requested designer Daiki Ozaki to create a bar with a more fashionable interior that would target adults like him who desire to savour drinks in an exclusive setting and who appreciate Japanese traditions. It was also important to Yonezawa that authentic materials would be used for the design as much as possible.

The core of this striking interior is marked by a conspicuous wooden counter in a slightly distorted U-shape. In its centre stands a large, authentic camellia tree with a structure around it for storing glasses and bottles. Water that is illuminated from beneath flows under the upper part of the structure, creating beautiful silhouettes against the tree. The camellia tree has a deep meaning in Japanese tradition and is an aesthetic symbol of Japanese Wabi-sabi. Its branches are often used for the Japanese tea ceremony. Its handsome image is repeated on Japanese washi paper covering a wall at the rear of the bar. This interior also features an interesting integration of private lofts on different levels around the counter, with each having its own staircase, ensuring absolute privacy for the perfect date.

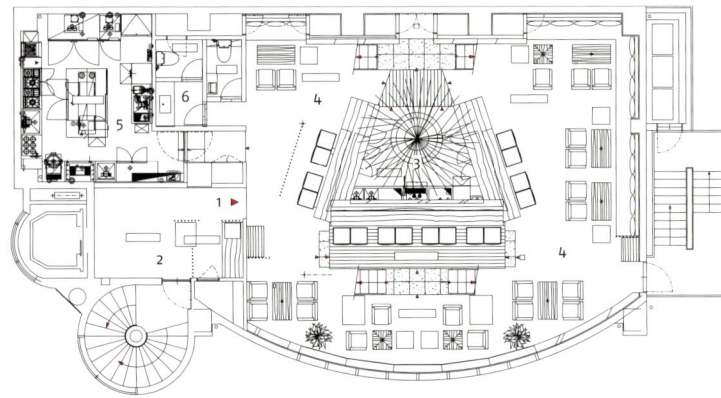

FIRST FLOOR

1 entrance
2 reception
3 bar
4 lounging area
5 kitchen
6 washroom

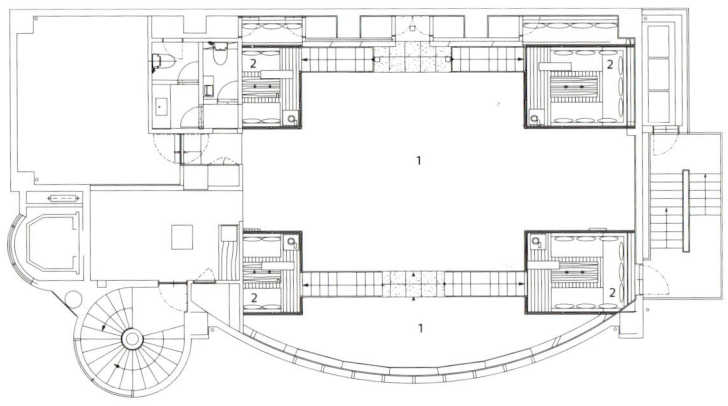

MEZZANINE LEVEL

1 void
2 lounging area

生命の大樹を囲み美酒を味わい、悠久に思いを馳せる夜。

PHOTOGRAPHY	Keisuke Miyamoto
DESIGNER	Myu Planning & Operators Inc.
DESIGN TEAM	Daiki Ozaki
CONTRACTOR	Arc Co., Ltd.
ADDRESS	2F, Ark Bldg., 1-17-1 Akita-machi, Tokushima City, Tokushima 770-0934
PHONE	+81 (0) 8 8655 3230
AREA	164 m²
SEATING	70 seats
COMPLETED	2005

東京 サンダーボルト

Thunderbolt

Maximum use of minimum space

Situated in Nakameguro, a district of Tokyo where many small individual bars are located, this inn is surely one of the most outstanding ones there. A huge thunderbolt on the façade greets the arriving visitors. On the day the owner Lupan signed the contract, he had yet to decide on the name of the bar. The weather was quite bad and when lightning suddenly struck, it was decided that the name of the bar would be "Thunderbolt".

The main visual feature of the bar is the spectacular painting of a dragon on the ceiling. The painting was the work of Holiyui, a professional tattoo artist and a friend of the owner. To avoid the practical difficulties of painting onsite, the work was completed before it was mounted. Since Lupan likes Japanese history, designer Yusaku Kaneshiro suggested using paintings of the Edo period for other design features. The god of lightning and the god of wind now rage on a panel behind the counter.

Lupan also requested that Kaneshiro integrate storage for a futon in the design, in case he had to sleep in the bar after closing hours. This was accomplished without losing precious space meant for customers, by using the space under an elevated niche where guests sit around a table. In fact, guests are more than happy to sit in an elevated area from which they can view the place. The only flaw is that women ought to be careful not to wear too short a skirt!

Since there is very little floor space, every inch is precious. Benches are designed so that they fit perfectly below the counter. These can be stowed away to make way for Lupan's futon.

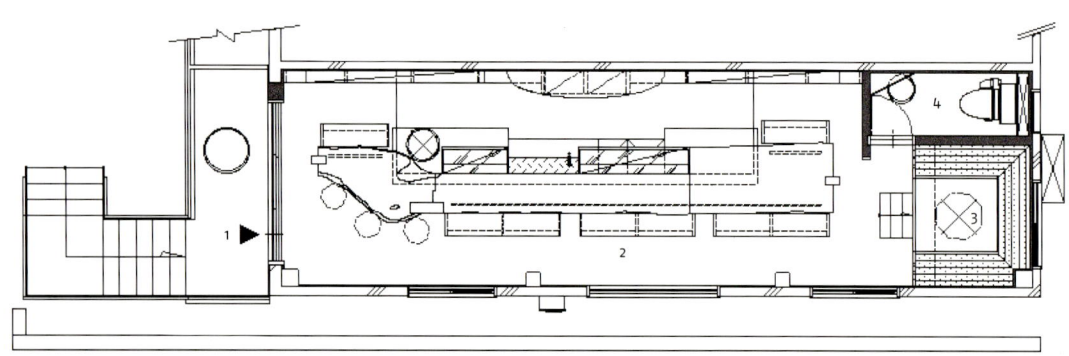

FLOORPLAN

1 entrance
2 bar
3 lounging area
4 washroom

風と雷と水の神々が織りなす夜は、ことのほか楽しい。

PHOTOGRAPHY	Masahiro Ishibashi
DESIGNER	Zoukei Syudan Co., Ltd.
DESIGN TEAM	Yusaku Kaneshiro, Mitsuru Komatsuzaki
CONTRACTOR	Lupin J. Hayama
ADDRESS	1-3-19 Kamimeguro SS Building 2F, Meguro-Ku, Tokyo 153-0051
PHONE	+81 (0) 3 6666 6773
AREA	33 m²
SEATING	21 seats
COMPLETED	2006

大阪 バー アール

Bar R

LED colours dance to your mood

To be able to enjoy the ambience of this private bar, guests have to either be friends of the owner or be introduced by them. The interior is truly magnificent, with what looks like many wolf heads staring down at the guests entering the bar. In reality, there is only one white wolf head that decorates the entrance area.

The most amazing visual feature of Bar R is a huge illuminated LED panel above the counter. The illumination can change into different hues, each looking as amazing as the other. If a guest has a special request, the bartender can change the hues at any time.

The chairs in front of the counter resemble grand antique remains from an old castle – in reality they are brand new, thought out by designer Hiroyuki Matsunaka, and made-to-order in China. With the huge cushion set in the backing, guests can spend the evening sitting very comfortably. These chairs are much more comfortable than a barstool, and far better looking.

The interior of the two private rooms, the King's Room and the Queen's Room, is equally impressive. In the Queen's Room, a beautiful shot of a woman with butterfly wings by photographer Hiroshi Nonami decorates the wall.

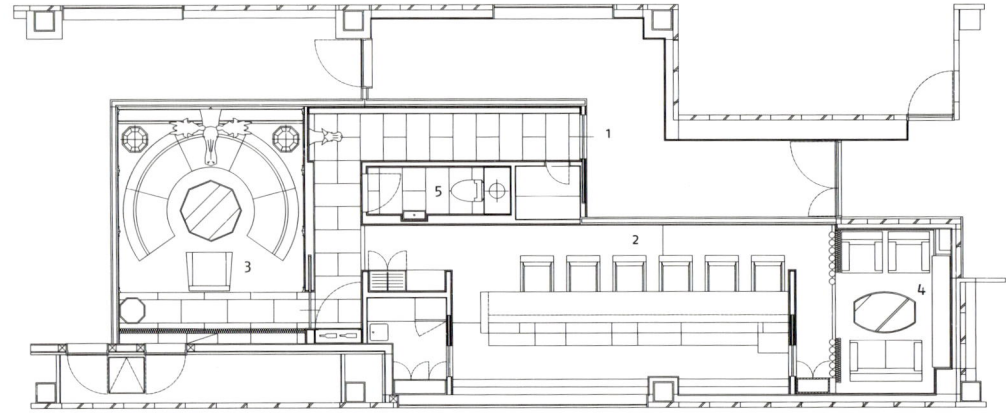

FLOORPLAN
1. entrance
2. bar
3. king room
4. queen room
5. washroom

酔うほどに幻想に誘引される、ここは時間のない世界。

PHOTOGRAPHY	Takeshi Nakasa (Nacasa & Partners Inc.)
DESIGNER	design room 702
DESIGN TEAM	Hiroyuki Matsunaka
CONTRACTOR	Ryuichi Morimoto
ADDRESS	2-8-6 Higashi-Shinsaibashi, Chuo-ku, Osaka 542-0083
AREA	66 m²
SEATING	20 seats
COMPLETED	2005

東京
ステア

Stair

Hidden treats from the terrace

Conveniently located near the trendy shopping streets of Aoyama and Omotesando, Stair is the perfect place to chill out after a long day of shopping. Since it is stowed away in a quiet side street, this bar lounge is never too crowded. It offers an atmosphere that is appealing and energising at the same time. Through the use of bright colours and graphic patterns, Wonderwall designer Masamichi Katayama has created yet another vibrant and unique interior.

The concept behind Stair's interior is the creation of a modern space similar to that of glittering cabarets in the past. Katayama's use of "calming" materials like marble or rosewood formed an ideal contrast to the tattoo-like serpentine pattern that slithers along the walls and ceiling, giving this place a distinctive character. Katayama assigned custom painter Masataka Kurashina to create the serpentine illustration "with a touch of mischievousness" after completing the interior.

Besides a semi-private room, there is a small terrace – a rare treat in Tokyo – that invites one to sit outside on lovely days. Sheltered by the roof, it can be used conveniently during rainy days – a great place for fresh-air fanatics. Artists and photographers can hire Stair for exhibitions or private parties that serve French fusion dishes and drinks. Equipped with a piano, Stair also hosts weekly jazz concerts, usually on Fridays.

柔らかな空間から生まれる、穏やかなで寛ぎの深い時間。

PHOTOGRAPHY	Ellen Nepilly
DESIGNER	Wonderwall Inc.
DESIGN TEAM	Masamichi Katayama, Masataka Kurashina (custom painting)
CONTRACTOR	At One's
ADDRESS	5-5-1 Minami-Aoyama, Minato-ku, Tokyo 107-0062
PHONE	+81 (0) 3 5778 3773
AREA	119 m²
SEATING	50 seats
COMPLETED	2005

東京

ウォータードロップス

Water Drops
Of wet, erotic glossy lips

This dazzling bar is located in Shinbashi, a district of Tokyo frequented by many middle-aged businessmen. Most bars and restaurants in this area are rather traditional and plain-looking, which makes Water Drops' stylish design particularly outstanding.

When designer Yukio Hashimoto creates interiors, he generally works in a very systematic and analytical manner. However, when he was asked to create an erotic design for this "girls' bar", he had the sudden image of red glossy lips and water drops in his mind. Lips have always been used as an erotic motif in the arts, but the way they have been integrated in the design of Water Drops is unique.

Hashimoto applied acrylic plates embossed with dots over the visuals of huge and glossy red lips on the walls, and over the windows at the front. With the right illumination, the dots come across looking like water droplets. Amplified through the use of polished black mikage stone, which has a strong reflective surface, the drops seem to echo all over the interior. Since the bar has only a space of 21 sqm, Hashimoto likens its interior to that of being in a glass with water drops covering its entire surface. With the low-key illumination and the contrast from the black flooring, ceiling and counter, the erotic red lips become very alluring indeed.

幾千の滴がたゆたう、煌めきと艶めきに包まれる夜。

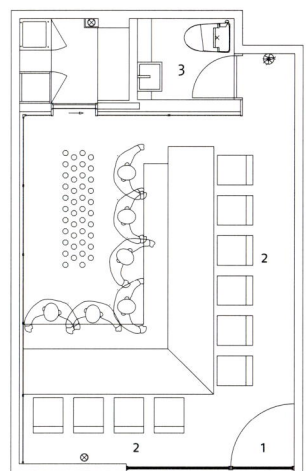

FLOORPLAN

1 entrance
2 bar
3 washroom

PHOTOGRAPHY	Ikunori Yamamoto (Nacasa & Partners Inc.)
DESIGNER	Hashimoto Yukio Design Studio Inc.
DESIGN TEAM	Yukio Hashimoto, Mariko Tachida
CONTRACTOR	Three O Inc.
ADDRESS	102, Shinbashi Kyodo Bldg. 3-11-5, Shinbashi, Minato-ku, Tokyo 105-0004
PHONE	+81 (0) 3 3438 1352
AREA	21 m²
SEATING	10 seats
COMPLETED	2006

Den Aquaroom

An oasis of tranquility

Located on two underground floors next to a congested crossing in Shinjuku, this bar is an oasis of tranquility. People who want to escape the incredible hustle and bustle of Tokyo will find the perfect space to relax in Den Aquaroom. Small groups of guests can watch the fishes in the showcase aquarium from their private rooms, although the larger open seating areas are just as comfortable and inviting.

Designer Daiki Ozaki experimented with different illuminations to achieve a special atmosphere for this interior. The soothing blue lights emitting from the fish tanks, the shining flames from the charming oil lamps, and the glow of the gas fireplace create a mix of entrancing, shimmering silhouettes reflected against the interior. The effect of the lights is especially enhanced by the white walls and dark flooring.

The staircase that leads down to the other basement level is no less eyecatching. White stairs with glass steps and the indirect illumination of the ground floor work to create an incredible impact. For guests passing the time over a glass of wine in Den Aquaroom, the experience is bound to be a soothing one, especially after a long and stressful day at work.

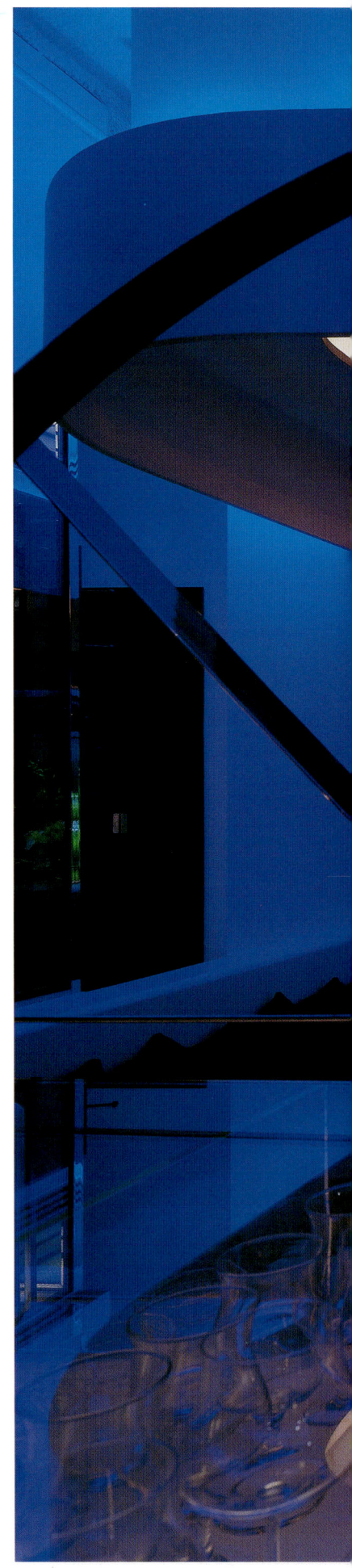

今宵、深海がもたらすのは、時間と重力のない世界。

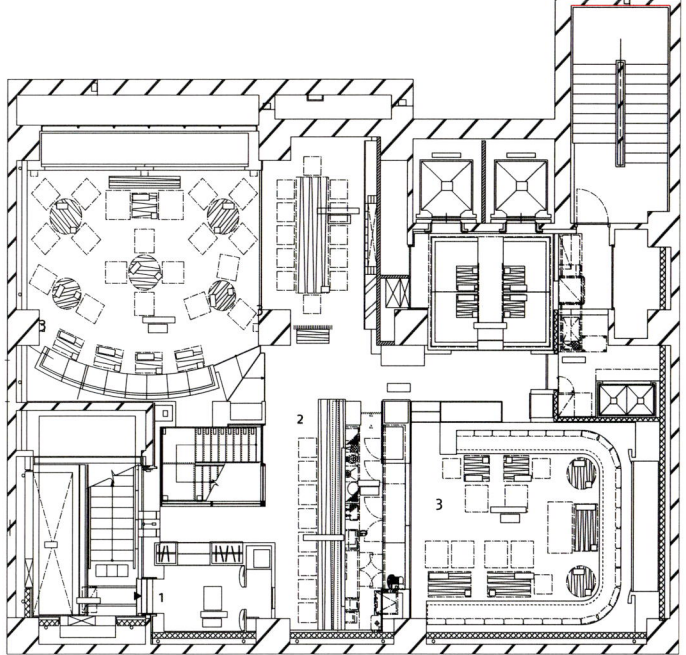

FIRST FLOOR

1 entrance
2 bar
3 lounging area

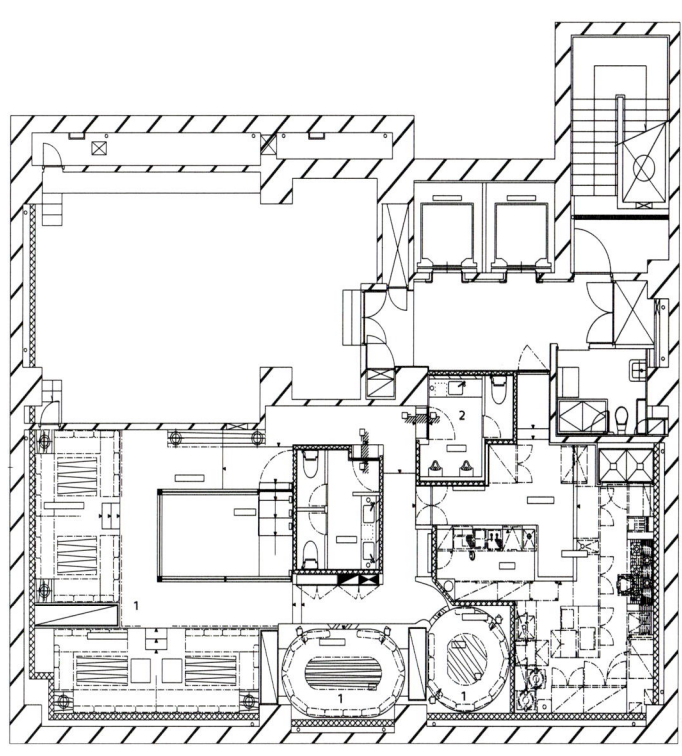

SECOND FLOOR

1 lounging area
2 washroom

PHOTOGRAPHY	Keisuke Miyamoto
DESIGNER	Myu Planning & Operators Inc.
DESIGN TEAM	Daiki Ozaki
CONTRACTOR	Myu Planning & Operators Inc.
ADDRESS	B1F/B2F, T&T Bldg., 3-32-30 Shinjuku, Shinjuku-ku, Tokyo 160-0022
PHONE	+81(0) 3 5367 4123
AREA	258 m²
SEATING	120 seats
COMPLETED	2003

仙台

シヅク トウヤ

Shizuku To Ya

Ripples in a pond

Sendai is located in the northeastern part of the Japanese main island Tohoku and is the capital of Miyagi Prefecture. The city of about one million inhabitants is well-known for its beautiful scenery. It is located about two hours away from Tokyo by Shinkansen.

Located in a district of Sendai called Kokubuncho is a series of three establishments belonging to the same owner. Each one is located within just one or two minutes by foot from the other, and all have "To Ya" as part of their names. The first two that designer Miki Orihara created had different concepts, and both enjoyed great success with customers. Hence, when the owner asked her to create a third one, Orihara felt great pressure, since the new design would have to be different from the others and still meet the expectations of both the owner and the customers. Her concern was unfounded; she did such a wonderful job that it won her a design award from the Japanese Society of Commercial Space Designers in 2006.

Orihara's client believes that premium alcohol can only be brewed with really pure water, and when she was discussing the design with him, he mentioned the keyword "Shitsuku" which means "droplet" in Japanese. Thus, droplets became the theme for the interior. Because it can also be spelled as "Shizuku", which is synonymous with the Japanese word for "service", the perfect name for this bar was found.

The drop patterns on the wall behind the counter are truly outstanding, serving equally well as drawers in which bottles can conveniently be stored out of sight. Even the plates are formed like droplets, while the round pattern on the hallway floor resembles ripples in a pond.

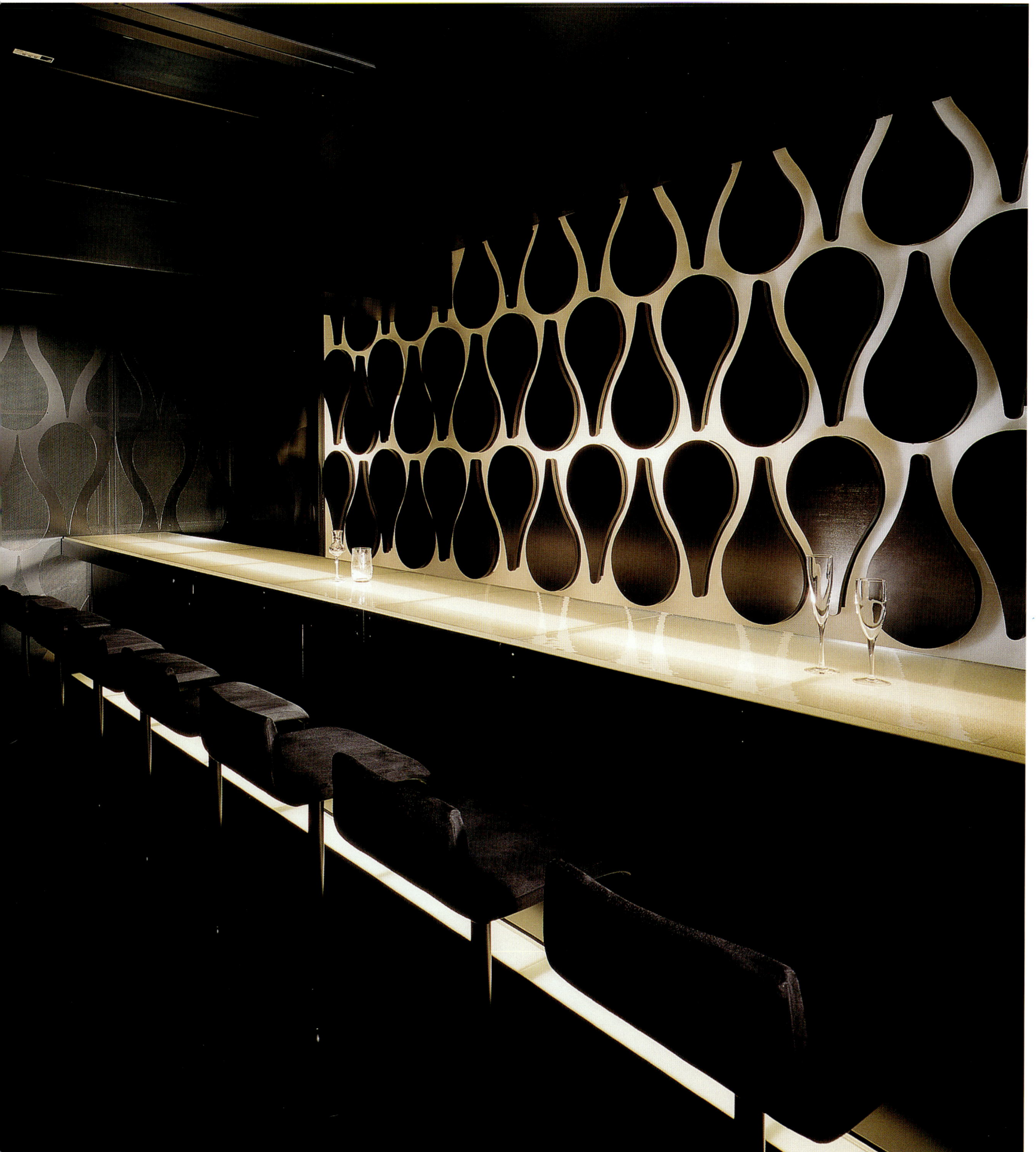

水音を感じる、水滴が煌めきをつくる、ここは雫という場所。

PHOTOGRAPHY	Setsuo Hirosaki (Vista Japan)
DESIGNER	Art • Form
DESIGN TEAM	Miki Orihara
CONTRACTOR	Grow Up Scene
ADDRESS	Aoba-ku, Sendai City 980-0811
PHONE	+81 (0) 2 2711 1644
AREA	106 m²
SEATING	30 seats
COMPLETED	2006

沖縄

山崎 *Yamazaki*

The ultimate symbol of femininity

Okinawa Island is situated between Japan's Kyushu Prefecture and Taiwan in the East China Sea. It is by far the biggest island in Okinawa Prefecture, which consists of approximately 160 islands, of which only 49 are inhabited. With its blue ocean, beautiful beaches, and warm friendly people, it is no surprise that the former Ryuku Kingdom became a popular travel destination in the region. Naha is the capital of Okinawa Prefecture and it is where Yamazaki, named after a famous Japanese whiskey brand, is located.

Although currently based in Tokyo, designer Yusaku Kaneshiro, who was born in Okinawa, is often called home to impress Okinawans with another one of his imaginative creations. When Kaneshiro was asked to design this "girls' bar", he came up with the idea to construct a counter shaped like a womb. He had seen a similar image at the entrance of an ancient Okinawan tomb. Yamazaki's counter, which surrounds the female bartenders, symbolises femininity and the womb from which they were born. The focal point of the interior is a pillar-like creation that goes up to the ceiling, where it is enlarged with mirrors. It can be illuminated with the chandeliers hanging within it. Yamazaki's customers are typically businessmen and women stopping by for a drink after work.

煌めきと輝きを囲い集う夜は、人をいつしか饒舌にする。

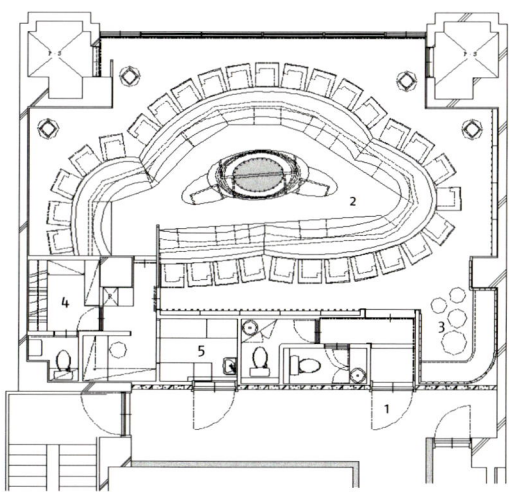

FLOORPLAN

1 entrance
2 bar
3 lounging area
4 staff room
5 washroom

PHOTOGRAPHY	Masahiro Ishibashi
DESIGNER	Zoukei Syudan Co., Ltd.
DESIGN TEAM	Yusaku Kaneshiro, Hiromi Sato
CONTRACTOR	Art Grover
ADDRESS	Okinawa-Suntory Bldg. 4F, 2-1-15 Matsuyama, Naha City, Okinawa 900-0032
PHONE	+81 (0) 9 8863 7260
AREA	95 m²
SEATING	35 seats
COMPLETED	2005

東京

竜宮の扉

Blue Lounge

Submerged in the depths of the sea

Designer Katsunori Suzuki's idea for the interior of Blue Lounge was inspired by a Japanese children's story about a fisherman named Urashima Taro, who saved a turtle on the beach from being tormented by children. In appreciation, the turtle invited him to Ryugu-jo, the Dragon King's palace in the depths of the sea. The fisherman spent many happy days in the palace before going back to shore, but upon returning home, he found that many decades had passed in his world. Everything was different and the people in his village were all gone, replaced by their descendants.

Blue Lounge attempts to recreate the magic of the Dragon King's palace. Unlike other aqua bars where seats are arranged facing the aquariums, Suzuki designed Blue Lounge so that guests are seated with their backs facing the tanks. Guests feel like they are surrounded by water on their comfortable dark blue velvet settees. The semi-circular arrangement of the aquariums and the use of mirrors create the sensation of being submerged underwater. The dim lighting and small interior with dark blue curtains that reach up to the ceiling reinforce the illusion. There is a cosy feeling similar to that of lying on a luxurious bed, except there are no fishes to watch.

Blue Lounge is conveniently located on the same level with three other restaurants in the building, providing guests with the perfect place to have a drink after dinner.

藍より出ずる青を愛で、今宵、その思いを語りあう。

FLOORPLAN

1　entrance
2　bar
3　lounging area
4　washroom

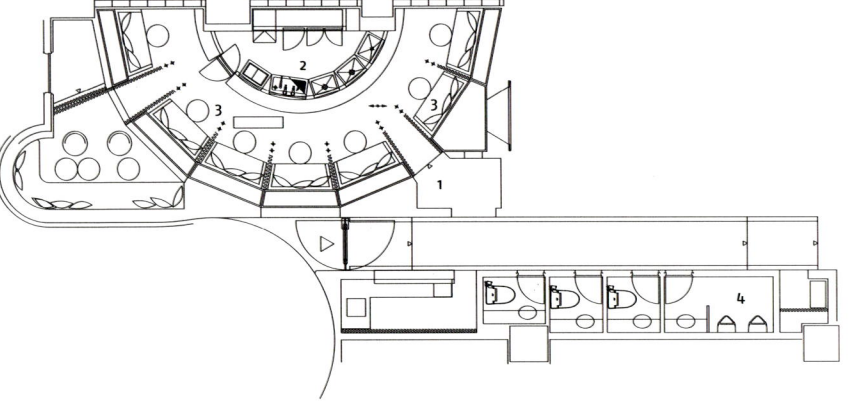

PHOTOGRAPHY	Ellen Nepilly
DESIGNER	Fantastic Design Works
DESIGN TEAM	Katsunori Suzuki
CONTRACTOR	Diamond Dining
ADDRESS	Fujikyu Building East Building No.3 B1F, 2-16-8, Minami-Ikebukuro, Toshima-ku, Tokyo 171-0022
PHONE	+81 (0) 3 3985 2194
AREA	50 m²
SEATING	20 seats
COMPLETED	2005

Ku-zu-ku

A façade of dried squids

This two-storey building hosts two establishments belonging to the same owner: Ikayakiyamagen Restaurant on the first, and Ku-zu-ku Bar on the second. "Ikayaki" literally means "grilled squid" in Japanese and refers to a particular food culture that started with food stalls in Osaka and other cities in the Kansai region. Unlike the "ikayaki" that can be bought in Tokyo, the "ikayaki" in Osaka is served with eggs and is closer to an omelette.

In Japan, it is common for people to eat snacks with alcohol. There are all kinds of different dishes to accompany drinks. The owner of this Osaka restaurant-bar has a special affection for ikayaki. He wanted to share his favourite food with guests and at the same time make this delicious snack more popular.

To emphasise that the restaurant's main dish is squid, and to inject a bit of humour, designer Akitoshi Imafuku used real dried squids for the design of the upper front of the building. Coated and attached in rows that adorn the façade, passersby often take a second look because they cannot believe their eyes.

The bar on the second floor probably possesses the most unique counter ever constructed. The concept of the design is "sora", the Japanese character for "sky", which was also used for the name of the bar. It was felt that there should be a division between the space above and below in the room. To communicate this, seats are built such that guests need to dive down, sit and put their head out of a square opening. Although this is a little inconvenient initially, the feeling of being virtually surrounded by a counter while sitting down is certainly a special experience.

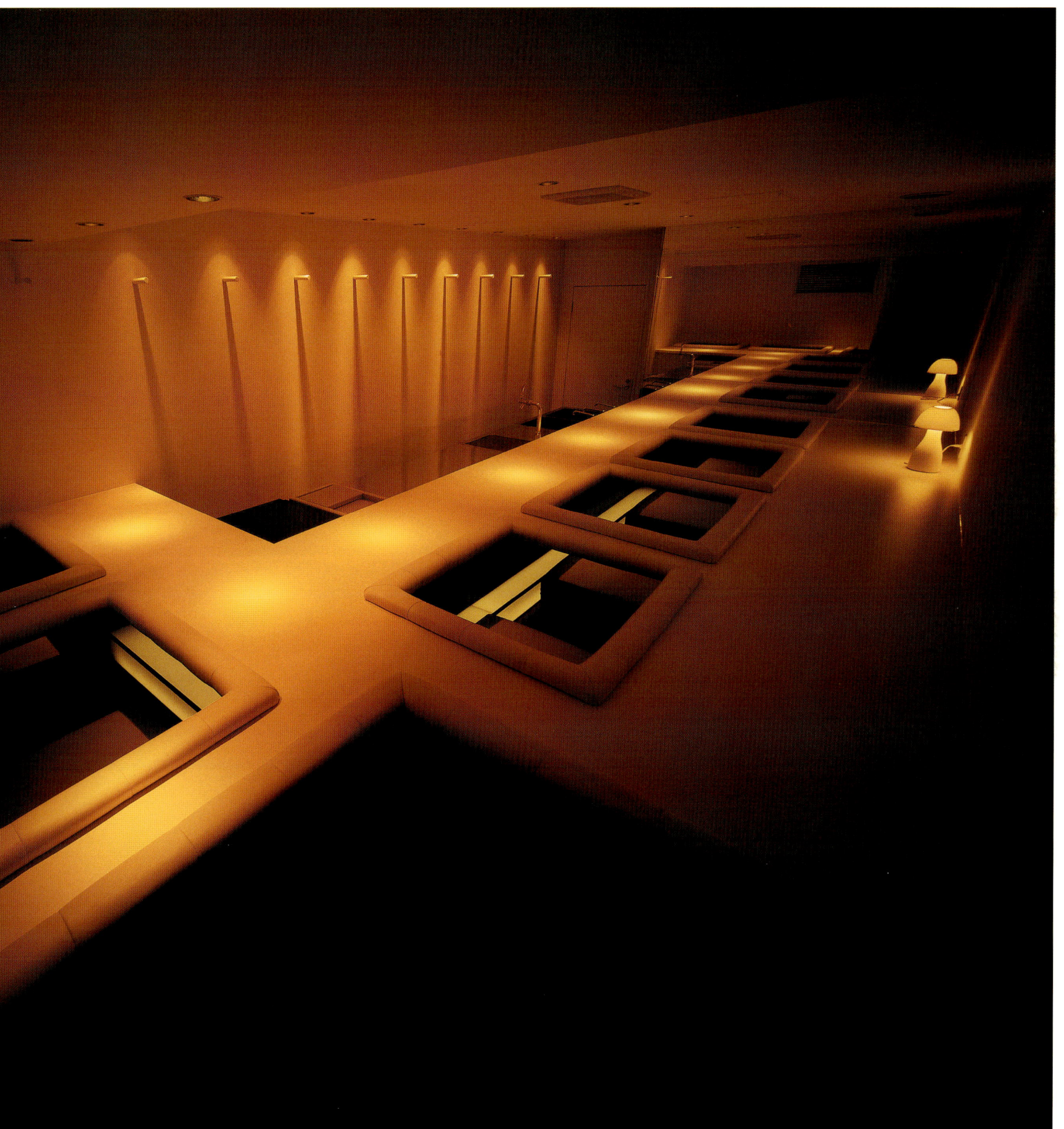

それは、雲の上のような空間、夢のような時間。

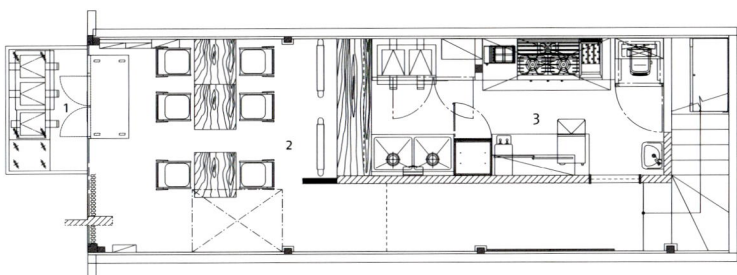

FIRST FLOOR
1 entrance
2 dining area
3 kitchen

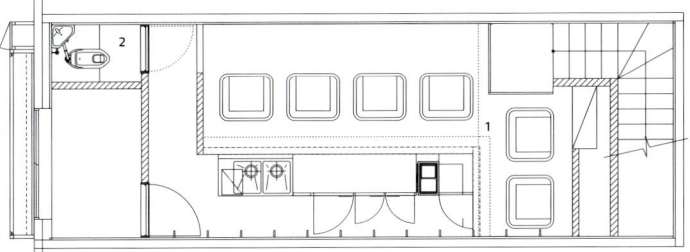

SECOND FLOOR
1 lounging area
2 washroom

PHOTOGRAPHY	Yoshihisa Araki
DESIGNER	Supermaniac Inc.
DESIGN TEAM	Akitoshi Imafuku
CONTRACTOR	Yamagen Co., Ltd.
ADDRESS	5-2-28 Higashi-Nodamachi, Miyakojima-ku, Osaka 534-0024
PHONE	+81 (0) 6 6358 7451
AREA	58 m²
SEATING	6 seats, 4 standing
COMPLETED	2007

Mission

The golden winged lion

Osaka City, with a population of about 2.7 million, is Japan's third largest city after Tokyo and Yokohama. It is also the home of this distinctive kyabakura known as Mission. Osaka has long been the cultural centre and economic powerhouse of the Kansai region. The city is known for its bustling nightlife, great food, and its people (who are apparently different from their Tokyo counterparts).

The club's moody black furniture and interior make the sparkling golden decoration stand out even more. Designer Katsuya Iwamoto's goal was to design a space that is classic but unusual. He felt that it had to be classic on one hand, but also illusory on the other, achieved through the use of modern lighting. Mission's interior would be light and simple but nevertheless gorgeous.

The focal point of the interior is a roaring golden winged lion standing on a wall, which looks like an elaborate prop from a fantasy film set. Behind it, mirrors in golden frames adorn the wall, reflecting the image of the winged creature.

黄金の獅子が出迎える空間で、漆黒と輝きに包まれる。

PHOTOGRAPHY	Seiryo Yamada
DESIGNER	Katsuya Iwamoto
DESIGN TEAM	Katsuya Iwamoto + Embody Design Association
CONTRACTOR	Eternal Corporation
ADDRESS	8-5, Kyoguchi-machi, Takatsuki-shi, Osaka 569-0072
PHONE	+81 (0) 7 2670 6888
AREA	198 m²
COMPLETED	2006

東京

水響亭

Suikyo-Tei

A river runs through it

When designer Yukio Hashimoto watched Andrei Tarkovsky's "Solaris", he was very impressed by one particular scene in which the astronaut visits the planet Solaris. In this scene, the lead character's house emerges from the Solaris ocean, looking exactly the way he had remembered it on Earth.

Drops of water drips off this image. Hashimoto said he had never seen such a wonderfully poetic scene before, and he knew that he would try to express what he had seen in an interior he would design some day. He successfully realised his wish with Suikyo-Tei.

Hashimoto integrated both real water and the image of water into the interior design. The floor was made to look as if a river ran through the establishment through the use of projection, giving guests the impression that they were walking over a river. In one of the private rooms, the tables look as if a water stream flowed inside them. Yet another room has a glass floor that looks as if it was built over a pool. With the approach towards integrating water into a space where it would not normally be expected, Hashimoto wanted to create a whole new emotional experience.

深海の碧に染められた夜更けに、時を忘れ心を浮遊させる。

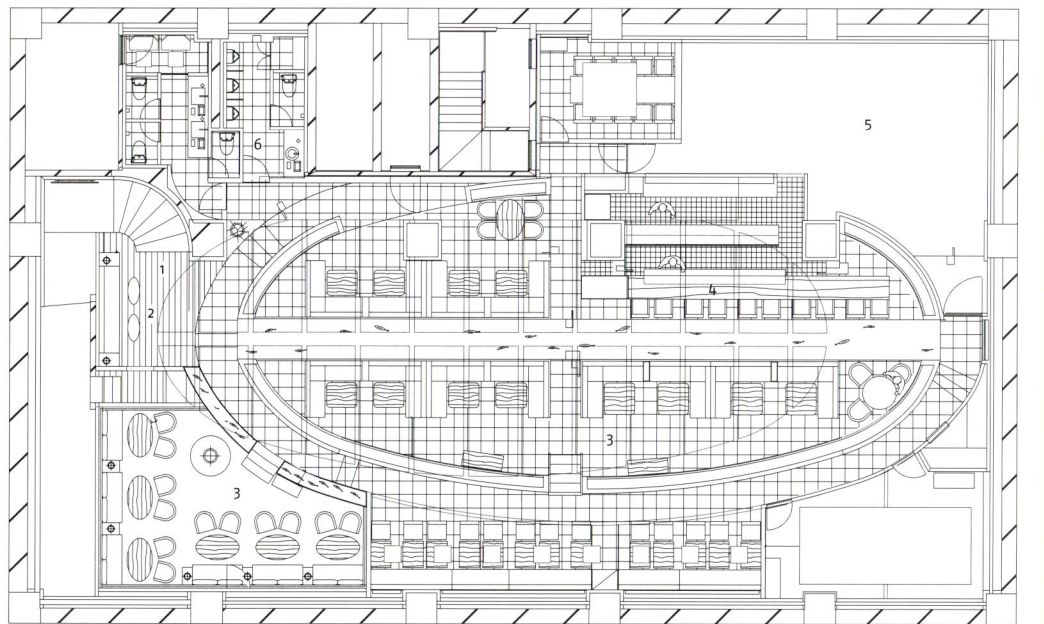

FLOORPLAN
1 entrance
2 reception
3 lounging area
4 bar
5 kitchen
6 washroom

PHOTOGRAPHY	Jun Nakamichi (Nacasa & Partners Inc.)
DESIGNER	Hashimoto Yukio Design Studio Inc.
DESIGN TEAM	Yukio Hashimoto, Shinichi Matsumoto
CONTRACTOR	Dynac Co. Ltd
ADDRESS	B2F, Mouri Bldg., 7-5-4, Ginza, Chuo-ku, Tokyo 104-0061
PHONE	+81 (0) 1 2033 8368
AREA	487 m²
SEATING	150 seats
COMPLETED	2004

横浜

ゆるり

Yururi

Seeking shelter in the wings of butterflies

Yururi is one of those establishments that Yusaku Kaneshiro designed to remind you of a scene from a fantasy movie. Entering the dining area, one almost expects Alice to appear in this modern wonderland. Structures resembling beautifully coloured butterfly wings enclose private seats for couples. With illumination from below, the acrylic wing structures transmit some of the light, creating an extraordinary and colourful atmosphere without being too flashy.

In another part of the premises, guests can walk up a flight of stairs to get into a huge "spaceship" where larger groups can enjoy their evening. Yururi is designed with an open-concept style, so that guests can enjoy the whole atmosphere of the striking interior from their seats.

The dim lighting and earthen colours create a relaxing atmosphere in which busy urbanites can temporarily forget about all the stresses of daily work. Located in Sakuragicho, the glittering waterfront district of Yokohama, the place is easily accessible to Tokyoites. Some seats are arranged so that guests can enjoy the amazing night view of the surroundings, including the giant Ferris wheel nearby. If guests are tired of looking out the window, they can gaze down at the glass floor below, where white sand circles that look like Zen gardens are sealed and protected under the glass tiles. These were created by young designer Mituru Komatzusaki, a member of Kaneshiro's team. Rose buds that emblazon the centre of the circles add final touches of refinement. Kaneshiro joked in an interview that only an earthquake would cause any damage to the designs.

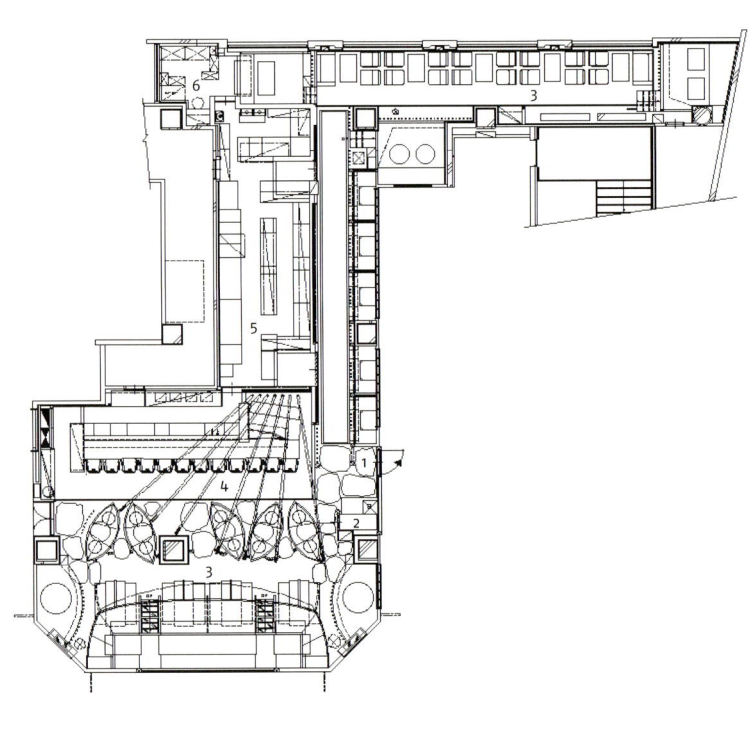

FLOORPLAN
1 entrance
2 cashier
3 lounging area
4 bar
5 kitchen
6 staff room

虹色の蝶が舞い降りた空間は、豊かで軽やかな時間が漂う。

PHOTOGRAPHY	Masahiro Ishibashi
DESIGNER	Zoukei Syudan Co., Ltd.
DESIGN TEAM	Yusaku Kaneshiro, Mitsuru Komatsuzaki
CONTRACTOR	Yamaji Food
ADDRESS	Cross Gate 4F, 1-1-67 Sakuragi-cho, Naka-ku, Yokohama City, Kanagawa 231-0062
PHONE	+81 (0) 4 5640 3577
AREA	225 m²
SEATING	129 seats
COMPLETED	2003

Restaurants
ADDRESSES

レストラン

008	VELOURS
014	LE BARON DE PARIS
020	ABSOLUT ICEBAR
024	DANCETERIA SAZAE
028	KITA AOYAMA SALON
032	REMIX
036	BIRTH
040	MINERVA
044	SHICHI-ZO
048	ZAZZLE
052	SHIMURAYA
056	AMEBAR
060	LIVE & BAR 11
064	ZODIAC
068	LE CABARET
074	CLUB ZOO
080	EURO CAFÉ
084	ROSA
088	SEASIDE
092	SAKURAJI
098	B BAR UMEDA
104	ESTASI
108	CLUB BISSER
114	LE CINQ
118	LUXE BAR EATS
124	THUNDERBOLT
130	BAR R
136	STAIR
142	WATER DROPS
146	DEN AQUAROOM
152	SHIZUKU TO YA
156	YAMAZAKI
160	BLUE LOUNGE
164	KU-ZU-KU
168	MISSION
174	SUIKYO-TEI
180	YURURI

107-0062東京都港区南青山6丁目4-6オルモストブルー地下1F
108-0072東京都港区南青山3-8-40青山センタービルB1F
150-0000東京都港区西麻布4-2-4 The Wall
530-0013大阪府北区茶屋町16-4
107-0061東京都港区北青山2−7−18 B1F
567-0821大阪府茨木市末広町2-27 2F
106-0031東京都港区西麻布2-24-12 B1F
605-0827京都市東山区八坂新地富永町106-4
271-0092千葉県松戸市松戸177 2F マチビル
106-0031東京都港区西麻布3-17-20 B1F
103-0013東京都中央区日本橋人形町2-20-7
150-0043東京都渋谷区道玄坂1-18-8道玄坂プラザ仁科屋ビ3F
542-0086大阪市中央区西心斎橋1-4-5御堂筋ビル11F
532-0011大阪市淀川区西中島3-13-8北中ビル3F
541-0053大阪市中央区本町4-5-4
542-0083大阪市中央区東心斎橋2-7-18暫ビル2F
662-0051兵庫県西宮市羽衣町5-12 1F 夙川プレイスビル
920-0847石川県金沢市堀川町3-111 7F
220-0005神奈川県横浜市西区南幸1-12-9 3F
663-8184兵庫県西宮市鳴尾町5-7-12
530-0001大阪市北区梅田1-8-16 ヒルトンプラザイースト 2F
605-0073京都市東山区祇園町北側347-91
104-0061東京都中央区銀座8-6-21ウォータービル2F
542-0083大阪市中央区東心斎橋1-19-15 鰻谷ブロックB1F
770-0934徳島県徳島市秋田町１-１７-１アークビル２F
153-0051東京都目黒区上目黒1-3-19上目黒SSビル 2階右
542-0083大阪市中央区東心斎橋2-8-6
107-0062東京都港区南青山5-5-1
105-0004東京都港区新橋3-11-5新橋共同ビル102
160-0022東京都新宿区新宿3-32-10 T&TビルB1〜B2
980-0811宮城県仙台市青葉区一番町4-4-5八百善ビルB1F
900-0032沖縄県那覇市松山2丁目1-15 サントリービル 4階
171-0022東京都豊島区南池袋2-16-8藤久ビル東３号館B1
534-0024大阪市都島区東野田町5-2-28
569-0072大阪府高槻市京口町8-5
104-0061東京都中央区銀座7-5-4、毛利ビルB2F
231-0062神奈川県横浜市中区桜木町1-1-67クロスゲート 4階

Architects & Designers INDEX

デザイナー

008	VELOURS
014	LE BARON DE PARIS
020	ABSOLUT ICEBAR
024	DANCETERIA SAZAE
028	KITA AOYAMA SALON
032	REMIX
036	BIRTH
040	MINERVA
044	SHICHI-ZO
048	ZAZZLE
052	SHIMURAYA
056	AMEBAR
060	LIVE & BAR 11
064	ZODIAC
068	LE CABARET
074	CLUB ZOO
080	EURO CAFÉ
084	ROSA
088	SEASIDE
092	SAKURAJI
098	B BAR UMEDA
104	ESTASI
108	CLUB BISSER
114	LE CINQ
118	LUXE BAR EATS
124	THUNDERBOLT
130	BAR R
136	STAIR
142	WATER DROPS
146	DEN AQUAROOM
152	SHIZUKU TO YA
156	YAMAZAKI
160	BLUE LOUNGE
164	KU-ZU-KU
168	MISSION
174	SUIKYO-TEI
180	YURURI

DESIGN ROOM 702, NAKAZAWA-KRAKI BUILDING 5E., 1-14-26, MINAMI-HORIE, NISHI-KU, OSAKA 550-0015

DESIGN ROOM 702, NAKAZAWA-KRAKI BUILDING 5E., 1-14-26, MINAMI-HORIE, NISHI-KU, OSAKA 550-0015

JENS THOMS IVARSSON - THOMS & NILSSON AB, STIGBERGSLIDEN 5, SPECKK, SE-414 63 GOTHENBURG, SWEDEN

CAFÉ CO., SIX BLDG 2-11-13 MINAMIHORIE NISHI-KU OSAKA 550-0015

LINE.INC., TRANSIT GENERAL OFFICE.INC, 5-5-10-202 MINAMI AOYAMA, MINATO-KU, TOKYO 107-0062

EMBODY DESIGN ASSOCIATION, 2F, 1-1-11 LABEL BLDG. NISHITENMA, KITA-KU, OSAKA 530-0047

FANTASTIC DESIGN WORKS, 401 MAISON MINAMI-AOYAMA, 5-18-4, MINAMI-AOYAMA, MINATO-KU, TOKYO 107-0062

HASHIMOTO YUKIO DESIGN STUDIO INC, 4-2-5, SENDAGAYA, SHIBUYA-KU, TOKYO 151-0051

BAYLEAF INC., 3F 12-19 DAIKANYAMA-CHO, SHIBUYA-KU, TOKYO 150-0034 & DESCARTES INC., 2F 2-4-10 SHIBUYA SHIBUYA-KU, TOKYO 150-0002

PROSTYLE DESIGN CO., LTD, 2-9-10 4F JIYUGAOKA, MEGURO-KU, TOKYO 152-0035

SHIGEMASA NOI DESIGN OFFICE, TENJINBASHI 1-3-4, KITAKU, OSAKA 530-0041

FANTASTIC DESIGN WORKS, 401 MAISON MINAMI-AOYAMA, 5-18-4, MINAMI-AOYAMA, MINATO-KU, TOKYO 107-0062

CAFÉ CO., SIX BLDG 2-11-13 MINAMIHORIE NISHI-KU OSAKA 550-0015

SPACE PLANNING-LAR, UCHUKEIKAKU FLAT 3F, 16-8 ISHIGATSUJI-CHO, TENNOJI-KU, OSAKA 543-0051

SUGA ARCHITECTS OFFICE CO.,LTD., DIAMONT BLDG. 7F, AKASHIMACHI, 47 BANCHI, CHUO-KU, KOBE 650-0037

DESIGN ROOM 702, NAKAZAWA-KRAKI BUILDING 5E., 1-14-26, MINAMI-HORIE, NISHI-KU, OSAKA 550-0015

EMBODY DESIGN ASSOCIATION, 2F, 1-1-11 LABEL BLDG. NISHITENMA, KITA-KU, OSAKA 530-0047

EMBODY DESIGN ASSOCIATION, 2F, 1-1-11 LABEL BLDG. NISHITENMA, KITA-KU, OSAKA 530-0047

SUPERMANIAC INC., 3F 2-2-2 TENMA, KITA-KU, OSAKA 530-0043

ZOUKEI SYUDAN CO., LTD., ITOU BUILDING 2F,1-8-3 EBISU, SHIBUYA-KU, TOKYO 150-0013

KIMIAKI TAKAHASHI, NR. 35 KOWA BLDG. ANNEX, 1-14-15 AKASAKA, MINATO-KU, TOKYO 107-0052

KIS DESIGN ASSOCIATES, 4-2-18-601 MINAMI-SENBA, CHUO-KU, OSAKA 542-0081

DESIGN ROOM 702, NAKAZAWA-KRAKI BUILDING 5E., 1-14-26, MINAMI-HORIE, NISHI-KU, OSAKA 550-0015

DESIGN ROOM 702, NAKAZAWA-KRAKI BUILDING 5E., 1-14-26, MINAMI-HORIE, NISHI-KU, OSAKA 550-0015

MYU PLANNING & OPERATORS INC., 6F, AKASAKA-NAKANISHI BLDG., 4-1-33 AKASAKA, MINATO-KU, TOKYO 107-0052

ZOUKEI SYUDAN CO.,LTD., ITOU BUILDING 2F,1-8-3 EBISU, SHIBUYA-KU, TOKYO 150-0013

DESIGN ROOM 702, NAKAZAWA-KRAKI BUILDING 5E., 1-14-26, MINAMI-HORIE, NISHI-KU, OSAKA 550-0015

WONDERWALL INC., 1-21-18 EBISU-MINAMI SHIBUYA-KU, TOKYO 150-0022

HASHIMOTO YUKIO DESIGN STUDIO INC, 4-2-5, SENDAGAYA, SHIBUYA-KU, TOKYO 151-0051

MYU PLANNING & OPERATORS INC., 6F, AKASAKA-NAKANISHI BLDG., 4-1-33 AKASAKA, MINATO-KU, TOKYO 107-0052

ART・FORM, 4-3-3-1502 MONIWADAI, TAIHAKU-KU, SENDAI CITY 982-0252, TOKYO OFFICE: 8-4-7-6A AKASAKA, MINATO-KU, TOKYO

ZOUKEI SYUDAN CO.,LTD., ITOU BUILDING 2F,1-8-3 EBISU, SHIBUYA-KU, TOKYO 150-0013

FANTASTIC DESIGN WORKS, 401 MAISON MINAMI-AOYAMA, 5-18-4, MINAMI-AOYAMA, MINATO-KU, TOKYO 107-0062

SUPERMANIAC INC., 3F 2-2-2 TENMA, KITA-KU, OSAKA 530-0043 & BAYLEAF INC., 3F 12-19 DAIKANYAMACHO, SHIBUYA-KU, TOKYO 150-002

EMBODY DESIGN ASSOCIATION, 2F, 1-1-11 LABEL BLDG. NISHITENMA, KITA-KU, OSAKA 530-0047

HASHIMOTO YUKIO DESIGN STUDIO INC., 4-2-5, SENDAGAYA, SHIBUYA-KU, TOKYO 151-0051

ZOUKEI SYUDAN CO.,LTD., ITOU BUILDING 2F,1-8-3 EBISU, SHIBUYA-KU, TOKYO 150-0013

詩 *Poems*
TRANSLATIONS

008	VELOURS
014	LE BARON DE PARIS
020	ABSOLUT ICEBAR
024	DANCETERIA SAZAE
028	KITA AOYAMA SALON
032	REMIX
036	BIRTH
040	MINERVA
044	SHICHI-ZO
048	ZAZZLE
052	SHIMURAYA
056	AMEBAR
060	LIVE & BAR 11
064	ZODIAC
068	LE CABARET
074	CLUB ZOO
080	EURO CAFÉ
084	ROSA
088	SEASIDE
092	SAKURAJI
098	B BAR UMEDA
104	ESTASI
108	CLUB BISSER
114	LE CINQ
118	LUXE BAR EATS
124	THUNDERBOLT
130	BAR R
136	STAIR
142	WATER DROPS
146	DEN AQUAROOM
152	SHIZUKU TO YA
156	YAMAZAKI
160	BLUE LOUNGE
164	KU-ZU-KU
168	MISSION
174	SUIKYO-TEI
180	YURURI

JAPANESE AND WESTERN STYLES UNITE AND OLD MEETS NEW IN THIS UNIQUE AND EXTRAORDINARY PLACE.

EXPLORE YOUR OTHER SELF CAPTURED BY THE ARISTOCRACY FROM ANCIENT TIMES, IN A SPACE WHERE SCARLET AND JET BLACK UNITE.

LET'S SAVOUR DELICIOUS SPIRITS BORN IN NORTHERN SOIL, IN A WORLD OF BLUE ICE.

THE MAGNIFICENCE OF THIS SPACE IS OBVIOUS FOR ART AND MUSIC SWIRL AND CHARM AND STYLE UNFURL..

THIS PLACE REMINDS OF A FORGOTTEN CASTLE – HERE, PEOPLE MAY FIND TIME TO REFLECT.

THIS IS A SPACE TINTED IN PASSION AND PURITY YOU CAN TALK ABOUT THE FUTURE HERE.

GLITTERING TEXTURE MEETS THIS SPACE WHERE YOU SHALL FORGET THE TIME AND BE COMPLETELY RELAXED.

A GLITTERING EPOCH SO FASCINATING THAT IT CARRIES YOU AWAY.

THE COUNTER'S DANCING DRAGON'S MIGHT, CONTROLS THE MANNERS OF DRINKING IN THE NIGHT.

AN ATMOSPHERE CREATED WITH SCARLET RED THAT PRODUCES SOFTNESS AND RELAXATION.

THE WARMTH OF THIS VIBRANT SPACE THAT IS WRAPPED IN WOOD THAT MAKES ME FEEL SO GOOD.

NO SPACE COULD BE MORE CALMING WITH ITS SHINING GLOW OF BROWN SO FAIR AND SCENT OF GROWN-UPS IN THE AIR.

ENJOY A DARING NIGHT MAGNIFICENCE AND ELEGANCE FINEST RED AND SPARKLING WHITE.

A CHARMING MOMENT IS BORN UNDER THE TWELVE SIGNS OF THE ZODIAC.

GRAVITY AND TIME HAVE NO MIGHT, IN THIS WORLD THE DEEP SEA GIVES BIRTH TO TONIGHT.

BEYOND TIME, BEYOND SPACE FORGET THE EVERYDAY LIFE – DON'T WORRY ABOUT TOMORROW TONIGHT.

A DIFFERENT CULTURE JUST A FEW STEPS AWAY - THE JOY OF A EUROPEAN STREET CORNER.

BE ENWRAPPED IN A ROSE COLOURED SPACE TONIGHT AND TALK ABOUT YOUR THOUGHTS AND FEELINGS.

A BEWITCHING SPACE WHERE GLITTERING BUBBLES RISE TO THE SURFACE. A WATER FOUNTAIN SHOOTING TO THE SKY.

UP DOWN LEFT RIGHT - A PLACE WITHOUT BOUNDARIES – RELAX AND LET YOURSELF GO.

REFINED NOT EXTRAVAGANT, NOT GAUDY BUT ELEGANT - A CHARISMATIC SPACE.

THIS GRACEFUL PLACE BREATHES THE ATMOSPHERE OF A FORMER PERIOD'S SENSE AND BEAUTY.

RELAXATION AND TENSION DIVIDE THIS SPACE – HERE I NEED TO MAINTAIN A FLAWLESS APPEARANCE.

THE SPIRIT OF SIMPLICITY AND FORTITUDE. ENJOY YOURSELF WITH FINE QUALITY DRINKS IN A FINE QUALITY INTERIOR.

SAVOUR DELICIOUS SPIRITS SURROUNDING A NATURAL TREE AND THINK ABOUT LIFE.

ANCIENT GODS OF WIND, THUNDER, AND WATER – THERE IS NO NIGHT MORE JOYFUL THAN THIS.

GROWING INTOXICATION INCREASES ILLUSIONS IN THIS WORLD WITHOUT TIME.

BORN FROM A SOFT PLACE - A CALMING AND RELAXING MOMENT.

A NIGHT ENWRAPPED IN THE SHIMMER AND CHARM OF THOUSAND SWAYING DROPS.

CALMING LIGHT AND SCARLET'S DIGNITY GIVE BIRTH TO GAIETY.

EXPERIENCE THE SOUND AND SPARKLE CREATED BY WATER DROPS, THIS PLACE IS CALLED SHIZUKU (DROP).

A GATHERING OF SPARKLE AND SHIMMER TONIGHT, SUDDENLY THE AIR IS FULL OF TALKATIVE DELIGHT.

INDIGO OUTCLASSES BLUE FROM WHICH IT WAS CREATED LOVE THIS NIGHT AND TALK ABOUT YOUR FEELINGS.

LIKE A DREAMY MOMENT WHERE YOU SEE YOURSELF FLY SOMEWHERE ABOVE THE SKY.

BE GREETED BY A GOLDEN LION AND ENWRAPPED IN JET-BLACK AND SPARKLE.

THE NIGHT'S HUE IS LIKE THE DEEP OCEAN SO BLUE, FORGET THE TIME AND LET YOUR HEART FLOW.

RAINBOW COLOURED BUTTERFLIES FLUTTER ABOUT, THE ATMOSPHERE IS RICH AND LIGHT AND FILLED WITH DELIGHT.

謝辞 *Acknowledgements*

The creation of this book would not have been possible without the help of so many individuals. The author and the publisher would like to express our deepest gratitude to the designers for allowing us to introduce the great design of their creations to readers around the world. We want to say thank you, in particular to the architects, designers, owners, and public relations personnel who despite repeated requests for material and information have remained cooperative throughout.. Many thanks also to the photographers who have granted us the permission to use their photographs for this book.

We furthermore want to emphasize our appreciation to Junichi Yanagisawa, for taking time away from his busy schedule and a family to do the refined Japanese copywriting for this book.

As author of this book I want to especially thank Adelien Vandeweghe who designed this lovely layout together with editor Elaine Lee for their great teamwork. It has been a great pleasure to work with them. Furthermore, I want to thank my husband for his support and his patience with me and my strange working hours, and also all my Japanese friends for their unceasing encouragement and support despite my persistent questions about the Japanese language and culture.

Remark of the author:

There are different systems of romanizing Japanese characters. A name spelled Katsunori in this book might be spelled Katunori in other publications. Words like shochu may be written shouchuu, or even sotyuu, elsewhere. The romanization used in this book is the one most commonly used in modern publications. Names of individuals or companies received from designer's offices were not changed, and only addresses were standardised throughout the book.